A practical and must-read primer for anyone struggling with self-care and longing for soul care. Grounded in Scripture and her experiences as a Christian minister and professional therapist, McWilliams challenges us to better care for our thoughts, emotions, and inward experiences. She leads us on a journey toward establishing new, sustainable rhythms and a kind of self-care that restores the soul and enables us to live the fulfilling life that Jesus wants for us!

**TOM LIN**, president and CEO of InterVarsity Christian Fellowship

This book is not a book to read and put on the shelf. It is a treasure chest of valuable insights and teaching. It is a recipe book for the soul. It is a book for those who want to live a fulfilled life and don't know how to get there. This is a book for people who want help as they seek to untangle their thoughts and emotions, to learn from them, and to experience transformation.

Janice McWilliams offers her wisdom as a therapist and spiritual director against the backdrop of how Jesus responded to his own emotions. The book is full of Scripture, practical advice, and the perspective of an author who is authentically journeying with her readers.

**ALICE FRYLING**, spiritual director and author of *Aging Faithfully: The Holy Invitation of Growing Older*

*Restore My Soul* is a beautiful tapestry of wisdom woven with threads of spiritual guidance, honest assessments of our needs, psychological insights, and heartfelt personal stories of transformation. Janice McWilliams has captured something you may not even know you're longing for, but as you read this book, you'll come to know what it is, and you'll have practical and attainable steps forward to a more sustainable life.

MARILYN VANCIL, author of *Beyond the Enneagram: An Invitation to Experience a More Centered Life with God*

In *Restore My Soul*, Janice McWilliams has given us a gift: gentle, wise, biblical counsel on how to grow and thrive as thinking, feeling creatures. This book is as practical as it is insightful and comes at a time when many of us need a little restoration for our souls.

REV. DON EVERTS, author of *Discover Your Gifts: Celebrating How God Made You and Everyone You Know*

A holistic, practical guide to self-care! Janice does a wonderful job helping us rethink the importance of self-care and provides step-by-step instructions so that we can easily integrate these principles into our daily lives. A must-read!

DR. MARK MAYFIELD, author of *The Path out of Loneliness: Finding and Fostering Connection to God, Ourselves, and One Another*

# Restore My Soul

## Reimagining Self-Care for a Sustainable Life

### Janice McWilliams

A NavPress resource published in alliance
with Tyndale House Publishers

**NavPress ◢**

NavPress is the publishing ministry of The Navigators, an international Christian organization and leader in personal spiritual development. NavPress is committed to helping people grow spiritually and enjoy lives of meaning and hope through personal and group resources that are biblically rooted, culturally relevant, and highly practical.

**For more information, visit NavPress.com.**

The Team:
David Zimmerman, Publisher; Deborah Sáenz Gonzalez, Acquisitions Editor; Elizabeth Schroll, Copy Editor; Olivia Eldredge, Operations Manager; Libby Dykstra, Designer; Sarah K. Johnson, Proofreader

Cover photograph of circles copyright © MirageC/Getty. All rights reserved.

Author photo by Arpasi Photography, copyright © 2022. All rights reserved.

Some of the anecdotal illustrations in this book are true to life and are included with the permission of the persons involved. All other illustrations are composites of real situations, and any resemblance to people living or dead is purely coincidental.

For information about special discounts for bulk purchases, please contact Tyndale House Publishers at csresponse@tyndale.com, or call 1-855-277-9400.

ISBN 978-1-64158-461-6

Printed in the United States of America

| 28 | 27 | 26 | 25 | 24 | 23 | 22 |
|----|----|----|----|----|----|----|
| 7  | 6  | 5  | 4  | 3  | 2  | 1  |

*For my clients. It has been an honor to walk with each of you and witness your courage and growth.*

# Contents

# Introduction

*The journey of a thousand miles does not begin with one step.*
*It begins with a desire to be somewhere else.*

PETE PEARSON, MENTOR

As a therapist, I often hear clients complain that the thought of addressing self-care in a meaningful way is overwhelming. I always point out how exhausting the alternative is. Think about it: How much energy do you expend on tamping down emotions, ruminating, or worrying? How defeating and depleting is it to work on something for hours and feel like you've gotten nothing done? How is the strain of not connecting well with family or friends working for you? And what cost is there to having an anemic or stunted relationship with God? This is the stuff of exhaustion and burnout. Doing the work of learning how to practice soul-restoring, life-sustaining self-care may require intention and effort, but the result is freedom and energy! In the end, an unhealthy soul will exhaust you far, far more than a restored one.

The idea of a restored soul makes most of us remember Psalm 23:

The LORD is my shepherd, I shall not want.
    He makes me lie down in green pastures;
he leads me beside still waters;
    *he restores my soul.*

PSALM 23:1-3, NRSV (EMPHASIS ADDED)

The green pastures and still waters where the Shepherd leads his sheep make me think of our very practical needs: rest, safety, eating and drinking. Then there is the little phrase about the Shepherd "restoring my soul" (see verse 3). The meaning of this is so vast and deep! I think of movement from discouraged to encouraged, from fatigued to rested, from fractured to whole. The idea of a restored soul evokes a feeling of peace and steadiness that intersects with the deepest cravings of my spirit.

In his book *A Shepherd Looks at Psalm 23*, W. Phillip Keller explores this idea through his vocation as a shepherd.

> Now there is an exact parallel to this [restoring my soul] in caring for sheep. Only those intimately acquainted with sheep and their habits understand the significance of a "cast" sheep. . . .
>
> A cast sheep is a very pathetic sight. Lying on its back, its feet in the air, it flays away frantically struggling to stand up. . . . It lies there lashing about in frightened frustration.
>
> If the owner does not arrive on the scene within a reasonably short time, the sheep will die.[1]

The image of the "cast" sheep is rich, real, and a little too close to home. How often are we stuck on our backs, struggling mightily, with no clear idea how to help ourselves or access the help of the Shepherd? Scripture is clear that it is the Shepherd's work to restore souls, to put the sheep back on their feet. But I have become passionate about helping people learn about the reasons they keep finding themselves stuck in the first place. That's where my idea to reimagine self-care began. I wanted to help my clients see and believe that the best self-care addresses the way they manage their inner experiences moment to moment, hour to hour, and day to day—*before* they wind up helpless on their backs, struggling.

I've been an Enneagram enthusiast, student, and teacher for twenty-five years. You don't need to know the Enneagram to appreciate this book. But these sentences might make more sense to those of you who do: I experienced a breakthrough in understanding how we tend to wind up as stuck sheep when I took a course on stances and repressed centers from Suzanne Stabile. I realized that when it comes to life-sustaining self-care, we wind up struggling in unique ways depending on our repressed centers—which correspond to our Enneagram types and what she calls our *centers of intelligence* (whether we're in the head, heart, or gut triad and which center of intelligence is dominant and which is repressed).[2] It's far too much to fully explain here; the gist of the teaching is that some types are *thinking repressed,* some are *feeling repressed,* and some are *doing repressed* (see the appendix for more detail). In other words, different people have different challenges in regard to healthy patterns of thinking, feeling, or doing.[3]

This repressed-centers theory gave overwhelming validation to what I see in my office. Certain skills are especially hard for certain people, and without intentional effort, this may never change. This helps explain why so many of us get stuck in life patterns that keep us overwhelmed and exhausted. To be at our best, we need to think effectively, feel without resistance, and do things that reflect the way

3

we want to live. Self-care in each area means getting better at tending to ourselves in real time, as challenges arise. Certain chapters in this book may present greater challenges to you—and, therefore, may be the most important work for you to tackle.

The thoughts chapters (2–3) are designed to help you learn that self-care in this area involves recognizing unhelpful thought patterns and creating better ones in the moment, as they arise. The emotions chapters (4–5) debunk the idea that certain emotions are off-limits. They encourage you to experience the range of emotions and teach you how to respond well to them. The rhythms chapters (6–7) reveal that self-care means having good rhythms of moving fast and slow, of work and rest, modeled after the way Jesus lived. And the fulfillment chapters (8–9) bring these streams of focus—thoughts, emotions, and rhythms—together by helping you develop self-care patterns for a meaningful and fulfilling life.

There are two chapters on each topic. The first chapters on each topic answer the question *Why?* and make the case for the centrality of health in that area to one's overall self-care. The second chapters on each topic—the "essential skills" chapters—answer the question *How?* and give concrete ways to practice the skills that will help you grow in each area. I envision the book as a manual of sorts, a resource that you'll be able to return to over time to refresh these skills. There is no need to read the chapters in order; you can easily begin with the content that interests you most or that feels most relevant. You can return to the chapters that help you through various experiences and life stages. But I do encourage you to read all of it—even the sections that cover areas you perceive to be your strengths. I have yet to come across a person who wouldn't benefit from considering how to live better with their thoughts and emotions or how to create more soul-restoring rhythms. And not enough people have thought intentionally about how to live with more fulfillment in the hours and days of their lives.

My spiritual-direction and therapy clients have inspired me with their remarkable journeys of struggling and overcoming. It has been an honor to walk with each one, and their stories are reflected in this book. In order to protect their privacy and honor their confidentiality, many details (such as names, professions, ages, histories, and genders) have been altered. Most of the characters in this book represent composites of several people. The anecdotes are no less genuine, as so many people wrestle with similar inner tensions that leave them depleted.

I have walked with many of my clients as they have shifted from the idea that self-care is an occasional activity to the notion that it is a moment-to-moment, day-to-day endeavor. This journey moves them from an untenable and overwhelming life to a fulfilling, sustainable one—the life of someone with a restored soul. Nothing gives me more satisfaction than seeing that transformation take place. The journey to a restored soul involves starting to see your inner world more clearly and then learning to apply life-sustaining self-care. The themes that I've found to be most important to the process are reflected in this book.

I haven't held back in this book. I firmly believe that the ideas in it are keys to preventing being a stuck sheep and living with a restored soul instead. The skills in this book have proven critical to restoring weary souls and recovering an overall sense of well-being in my clients. In turn, my clients have been empowered to live the lives God has called them to. The better we are at life-sustaining self-care, the freer we will be to give time, energy, and talents to the things that matter in the Kingdom of God.

So, dear readers, I pray this book will move you from muddled to clear, from unstable to steady, from unsatisfied to fulfilled. For the sake of the gospel and our souls, let's live better.

Your efforts at self-care
are not having the
effect you want.

There is a better way
to understand self-care.

This book is your road map.

A sustainable, fulfilling
life is the goal.

# CHAPTER ONE

# Reimagining Self-Care

My friend Úna forwarded me the link with a text: "Did you know there is a line of self-care Barbies?!?!?" I was hard at work on this book at the time, wrestling with popular concepts of self-care, and the two of us had enjoyed several conversations on the topic. I quickly clicked on the link, and there she was: Barbie, in a pink bathrobe, with her iconic lipsticked smile. The play set had cucumbers to put on her eyes and Barbie dough, presumably to use for her facial treatments. I quickly texted back, "Oh wow, just . . . wow." By this time I was hooked, so I did a little more digging. The copy below the doll read, "The new line of the iconic doll has been designed to introduce girls to the benefits of self-care through play."[1] The doll is ready for the spa with a face mask and a puppy who is geared up for a spa day as well, with its own little eye mask resting on its head.

Cute.

But not helpful! Too many people are suffering from inadequate concepts of self-care, and they (and quite possibly you) are suffering as a result. Incidentally, a Google search of "self-care Ken" gets you nothing, reflecting the commonly touted idea that soul care and self-care are tasks that only women pursue or need. Our society's prevalent portrayal of self-care as merely skin-deep pampering and not applicable to men confirms my suspicion that self-care is a thoroughly misunderstood topic. Most men and women fail to recognize the most important aspects of self-care or that all of us need it to thrive. Most of us consider self-care when we are at the end of ourselves, exhausted and overwhelmed. We plan a day fishing or at the spa—great, restful activities—but then resume the life patterns that made us exhausted and overwhelmed! In my therapy practice, I have treated many dear clients who do a lot of Barbie-style self-care while their lives continue to disintegrate.

This makes me sad. You, dear reader, were not born for such a fate. Neither was I! John 10:10 tells us that Jesus came so that we might have "a rich and satisfying life," life to the full! Not an anemic and struggling life. Not an exhausted and depleted life. Not an overwhelmed and unfulfilled life. No! A rich and satisfying life. Barbie-style self-care isn't getting us there, and Jesus has so much to teach us. Jesus was an exceptionally healthy and balanced individual who was actively tending to his inner world, and we can learn from his example.

Puzzling over Jesus' life—his emotional health, his capacity to be busy, his ease in being slow, and the way he lived so focused and present—is what led me to this conclusion: Learning to care for our inner worlds (our thoughts, emotions, and inward experiences) in an ongoing way is the life-sustaining self-care that we need.

Thousands of hours of walking with clients have only added to my conviction. So, I've developed a bit of a bad attitude about what we typically think of as self-care and a wild passion for something deeper and more sustainable.

## Exhaustion in the Name of Service

A turning point in my understanding of the problem came when I was leading a self-care workshop for tired, discouraged, and dis-illusioned refugee-resettlement workers in an organization with shrinking funding. These caseworkers described their lives to me: erratic hours, bureaucratic obstacles, frequent tears, near-constant frustration, and tedious persistence in working within dysfunctional systems. Yet their own self-care stayed in the shadow of their incred-ible passion to attend to the needs of refugees. Most of them defined self-care as last-ditch efforts to prevent dropping from exhaustion or having health problems. And for some, self-care felt like a frivolous add-on that had no place in their lives of service. One worker shared,

> When I take care of myself, you know, watch shows or go to bed early, I just feel bad! Then I think that I deserve to rest, and I get mad at anyone who demands anything of me. I'm all over the place!

Another added,

> I am running all day long, fuming one minute, berating myself for my anger in the next, wanting to cry for the pain my clients are going through a few minutes later. I'm on the phone trying to get through to the right person at one agency while I'm waiting in line at a different agency with a client who's getting the runaround. The tasks never end, and every single one of them has gotten harder to accomplish. I want to scream half the day.

As I clicked through my slides and continued to listen, the challenge of a different mindset felt at once necessary and daunting. These dear individuals who were working so hard to fulfill a difficult call in their lives needed more than Barbie-style self-care. They needed to know how to manage their inner lives as they navigated the pressures and obstacles they encountered every hour of every day. They needed to learn to care for their minds and souls; that is what would empower them to love the refugees they served over time. How could they each learn to reframe their idea of self-care from one of selfish frivolity to moment-by-moment tending to their inner experiences? How could they learn to order their hours, days, and weeks so that their souls and bodies could enjoy some much-needed pacing? I felt my workshop was barely scratching the surface! Somehow, an unsustainable lifestyle had become the norm in their organization, without anyone setting out to make it that way. And that is true in businesses, family lives, and our society more generally—so much so that deciding what healthy expectations even look like is a major challenge!

I'm sympathetic to the confusion of expectations. Every time I get a call asking if I'm taking new clients, a dozen or so questions come to mind. *Have I felt too busy lately? Is my caseload too heavy?* I see other therapists answer this question definitively, and I marvel at how they respond with such ease. "I have one slot at 11:00 a.m. on Thursdays; will that work for you?" I wonder at the predictability of their clients and what in the world is wrong with mine . . . or rather, with me! *I don't require my clients to come at the same time every week. Should I? More often, our appointments roam around my schedule. And how many come on a weekly basis? Should I know that? Are these other therapists doing regular audits or something? Do they have this self-care thing in the bag? Am I just handling things wrong?* I'm convinced that none of us is immune to the challenge of boundaries and balance in work, family, and other responsibilities. I've yet to come across someone who couldn't do with some help.

## The Pressure to Never Slow Down

Cora is no exception. She's an executive at a successful, large business. I've been working with her for a couple of years, helping her process the many challenges of balancing an exceedingly demanding job with a home life. I'm reacting to her report of a recent day off.

"Wait, did you say you were submerged?"

"Yes, it's a floating rest pool."

"What does it do?"

"It accelerates rejuvenation."

"How?"

"Oh, I have no idea, but there's lots of research. And hey, if it's fast, I need it!"

"So you lie in it . . ."

"Yes, for thirty minutes."

"And . . . what?"

"It's supposed to be as helpful to your body as three massages and ten hours of sleep."

"Wow."

Cora is lit up, like she often is, explaining this to me. Our sessions are at 7:00 p.m., and she comes straight from the office. It often takes her half the session to stop vibrating from the relentless pace of her workplace. And I truly feel for her; her employer's expectations are intense, and quitting is fraught with complicated trade-offs. Cora is wonderful at what she does, but she seems to enjoy her job less and less. We've been talking for months about the quality and quantity of her sleep, among other things. I fear that Cora may think she has temporarily solved this problem with her thirty-minute float. As I consider how to continue, she absentmindedly reaches for her phone, checking the notification that has popped up on the screen.

"That can wait." She looks up from her phone. "Anyway, I couldn't spare the whole day . . . too much to do at home. So, speedy float it was!"

"Did it . . . work?"

"Oh, heck if I know! But I'm off the hook for self-care, right? At least for this week."

She gives me a wry, sideways smirk, knowing that I regularly bring this up. I worry that she is going to drop from exhaustion one day. Just when I think she cannot handle any more, another giant work project lands in her lap, or her husband gets demoted, or they lose a babysitter, or her father moves into a care facility. Cora just keeps going, and nothing seems to let up. Our conversations about self-care often devolve into a defensive "Well, I'm coming here, aren't I?"

In my weaker moments, I feel the responsibility of this phrase, as if the whole of Cora's self-care rests on me and our fifty-minute sessions. And, in a way, that's what Cora hopes. The "Well, I *am* seeing a therapist!" antidote for a jam-packed, frenetic, and relentless life feels like a huge commitment to someone like Cora. But when every day of Cora's life is a proverbial sprint triathlon, how can seeing me and spending thirty minutes in a floating bath really help? Cora needs to revamp how she lives her days so that she experiences something other than adrenaline-pumping high gear. She lacks pacing and rhythm in her life. The trouble is, she cannot bring herself to take time for even the shortest breaks or mindful moments. She fears backing off because one of the plates she's spinning may drop. And the messaging is abundantly clear: In her job, those who slow down are downsized.

## Self-Care, Barbie-Style

Cora is like many of us in thinking that doing a nice thing for herself constitutes self-care. It does! The trouble is, the floating pool isn't enough. Don't get me wrong; I'd rather her take the time to do that than do nothing at all, but she needs more. Several assumptions about self-care block the process of long-term life change. We get stuck when we assume that self-care that is practiced only sporadically or that only addresses one aspect of our lives is adequate.

Here are some common ways self-care gets reduced to a one-dimensional action:

- *"Me time"*: Self-care is seen as doing things to pamper yourself or engaging in a recreational activity, usually alone. Self-care is reduced to a way of justifying doing pleasurable things.
- *Emergency measure*: Self-care is understood as a measure to prevent catastrophic physical or emotional overload. Self-care is reduced to a last-ditch effort to survive.
- *Dieting*: Self-care is considered to mean giving up sugar, tackling whole-food nutrition, practicing time-restricted eating, doing a Whole30, or using one of countless food plans. Self-care is reduced to a consideration of the body.
- *Exercise*: Self-care is all about the "right" exercise program, which can mean anything from attending yoga class to training for a triathlon. Self-care is reduced to being in shape or expending energy.
- *Saying no*: Self-care is seen as developing one's ability to say no and create limits. Self-care is reduced to justifying the need for boundaries.

What I see is that very few people experience a balanced, flourishing life even if they are serious about one or two of these themes. And their attachment to any of these themes tends to make them feel that they've conquered self-care, even if gaping pockets of their lives remain out of control. Their souls are anything but restored.

## Life-Sustaining Self-Care

My conclusion? These self-care themes aren't enough. We need to learn how to live better in an ongoing way. I think of the man who is a rock star in terms of regular exercise and diet but who has no idea how to deal with his emotions. Or the woman who gets regular pedicures but is plagued with worry the better part of most days. We need a model that encourages the care of oneself in the moments and hours of everyday life instead of just an isolated day off work. Self-care needs to go beyond a one-dimensional concept like "me time," and it ought to consider the body and boundaries. It should involve both external practices and internal realities. Life-sustaining self-care implies a bigger picture that will result in better outcomes. I don't want to end another self-care workshop with the young-adult attendees still feeling stuck in cycles of *exertion* → *burnout* → *withdrawal* that they cannot break.

Life-sustaining self-care is a call to moment-by-moment, hour-by-hour, and day-by-day living where we are increasingly confident that we know how to handle everything that is happening inside us. We move away from a mindset of "paying our dues" with a one-dimensional, Barbie-style self-care measure like taking a spa day or doing a Whole30, and we move toward tending our inner experiences in a way that translates into overall spiritual and emotional well-being. We might still have spa days or do Whole30s, but only in the context of more consistent internal work. This internal work sets us up to live the way we want to in the world for the long haul: more like Jesus and less like our typical, modern-day, stressed-out selves.

## What is the difference between typical, one-dimensional self-care and life-sustaining self-care?

Here are just a few examples of how the difference may look or be experienced.

| ONE-DIMENSIONAL SELF-CARE | LIFE-SUSTAINING SELF-CARE |
| --- | --- |
| taking a vacation after a busy season at work to recover from burnout | knowing how to manage the internal challenges of each day during a busy season and then experiencing your vacation as true replenishment, not just recovery |
| scrolling through your phone for a quick break and suddenly realizing that forty-five minutes (that you can't spare) have passed | understanding the pull of the phone and staying aware of your time on it; having several ways to spend replenishing breaks |
| feeling desperate to have a couple of drinks to unwind | knowing how to manage emotions and having several ways to self-soothe; you can enjoy a drink or not |
| taking a day off due to feeling overwhelmed | knowing how to handle the range of human emotions and saving your day off for something enjoyable |
| distracting yourself with a movie to stop your mind from churning | dealing well with intrusive thoughts without needing to distract your mind; watching movies because you like them, not because you need an escape from your thoughts |

Self-care that restores the soul involves a commitment to caring well for our inner worlds. We learn to tend to our emotions, thoughts, pacing, and moods. In doing so, we address self-care at its roots and set the tone for personal thriving.

When we practice life-sustaining self-care, we feel capable of moving fast and slow. We know how to rest and how to press hard. We've learned what adjustments we need to make to move through seasons of intensity, struggle, and ease. We know how to develop rhythms in our days, weeks, months, and years. We can experience the range of emotions without becoming overwhelmed, and we know how to address unhelpful thought patterns. Ultimately, when we know how to deal with ourselves well hour by hour and day by day, we are far less likely to struggle week to week and month to month.

> Self-care that restores the soul involves a commitment to caring well for our inner worlds.

## A Sustainable Life

Graves is one of my clients who recently sharpened my thinking on living well with emotions. Since George Floyd's death at the hands of a police officer in 2020, Graves has been organizing, advocating, writing, speaking, and posting.

"I have to stay angry. Those who let up on their anger become complacent, and we can't do that again."

"So how does that work? How do you stay angry?"

"I stay on the chats with others who have been hurt by police. We have to pump each other up. I can't let down, not now."

"There's a difference between staying committed to the principles of justice and actually *feeling* angry in an ongoing way . . . Which do you mean?"

"I mean feeling angry. We have to stay connected to it, or we might lose momentum. I've seen it too many times."

As Graves shares, I feel viscerally challenged about how to proceed. He has numerous health issues, and I know statistics on the prevalence of early deaths due to said health issues in black men. The stress of racial injustice—in all its forms—is an underlying condition that wreaks havoc on the bodies of people of color, and Graves's ongoing weathering is taking a toll. I fear that sustaining anger for the length of time it will take for change to happen is downright dangerous for him. But he has named his dilemma: He doesn't know how his own efforts, or an overall movement, can keep momentum without anger.

"Graves, there has to be another way."

"Oh yeah? Tell me—what's the other way?"

His tone is challenging and skeptical. His response raises my fear that my own naïveté as a white woman makes even the idea of life without anger a posture of privilege in this country. I proceed tentatively.

"The world needs you for the long haul, Graves. Can we talk about you living your life, and therefore your emotions, in a way that enables you to keep going for the next twenty-five years? I don't want your body giving out. You're too important."

From there, we talked about important soul-restoring concepts: experiencing emotions, self-soothing, and refining values. Each of these concepts will be filled out in the following chapters and make up part of a critical whole. It's taking time, but Graves and I are partnering to reimagine a life in which he handles his anger well so that he will flourish rather than wear himself to exhaustion and perpetuate a system that has already cost him—and his body—so, so much.

## A New Landscape

Graves is not unusual. We are more stressed, more depressed, and less steady as a people than we have ever been. Everyone is trying to do life with a backdrop of unspeakable stress and uncertainty in the world—economically, politically, systemically, and environmentally. And we're facing a huge challenge: The role of the news cycle has taken on a whole new form, rising from unsettling to utterly destabilizing. In the face of such pressure, having the skills to manage our inner experiences has never been more critical.

"So, this was how long?" I ask my client, Yu-Shin, who is debriefing a day in her COVID life.

"I worked out for forty-five minutes. By the time I checked my phone, I had over one hundred texts from my mom friends. One of them shared an article about how bad virtual learning would be for social development or something. It started this whole wave of moms rethinking decisions, calling private schools, re-researching community centers that are hoping to have on-site experiences for children . . . I feel like if I don't freak out with them, I'm going to miss something critical for my own kids! I don't know how to stop jumping in."

She looks up into her camera at me through our screens and says, "And something like this happens almost every day! I feel like my blood pressure must be through the roof half the time. I hate reading all the texts and clips and articles, but I seriously cannot stop."

I shake my head sympathetically and wonder where to go next with our session. Yu-Shin's constant connection with these friends is at once her lifeline of support and the thing that escalates her stress. She is a follower of Jesus, but her steadiness moment to moment depends largely on what she sees on her phone. If good news is reflected there, she feels good. If the news is bad, she feels bad. We have worked on this with varying success over time, but the ever-changing news that so affects her day-to-day life has her more tethered to her phone than ever before.

## Jesus as Our Example

How would Jesus have handled stressors like this? In Mark 4, Jesus is taking a nap when a big stressor hits the disciples. Seriously, Jesus? The disciples are rattled and afraid as a sudden storm threatens to sink their boat. Jesus is able to sleep through the noise and seems unalarmed when very scared and resentful disciples wake him up. "Teacher, don't you care that we're going to drown?" the disciples ask (verse 38). Jesus amazes them by calming the sea. Underneath the working of this miracle is a decision *not* to react to everything that happens *when it happens*. How did Jesus do this, and what can we learn from his example?

Sometimes Jesus stayed focused in spite of circumstances, and sometimes he allowed himself to be interrupted. In the story of the bleeding woman in Mark 5, Jesus is headed to heal Jairus's daughter, who is near death. Yet when the woman touches him, he stops and listens to her story of twelve years of suffering. In some such instances, Jesus allowed the interruption and shifted his attention; other times, he didn't. How did he decide what to do? We don't know Jesus' thoughts on either of these occasions, but we have much to learn from the fact that he didn't always snap into action in response to new information. Jesus was *holding on to* his attention and energy—something that we rarely consider but that has the potential to transform our lives.

A soul-restoring model of self-care moves us toward a sustainable life rhythm. Jesus modeled a life of being very busy at times, guarding time for prayer at others, and having the energy and reserve to be interrupted and redirected on many occasions. I believe that his flexibility came from an overall well-being, which we should seek and emulate. Jesus' life and ministry show us that a well-managed life doesn't necessarily look predictable or overly rigid. He had long days of nonstop ministry and an intense travel schedule at times. But we also see him enjoying long meals, a slow pace, and special time with his closest followers. How did he do this? I believe Jesus knew something about life-sustaining self-care, and he did it well. Just consider what we *don't* see recorded in the Gospels. Jesus never

> falls apart emotionally,
> burns out,
> stays in bed all day,
> acts distracted and distant,
> becomes volatile, or
> succumbs to moodiness.

Impressive, isn't it? Jesus remained steady and openhearted at times most of us would shut down. Jesus responded to things with emotion and force, but he didn't lose control like we often do, with unreasonable ranting and yelling, collapsing into unexplainable tears, or shutting down. In his life on earth, Jesus showed himself to be a grounded and healthy person. We may be tempted to write him off as "too divine" to hold as a role model, but we are called to do just that. He lived a rich and satisfying life, and he wants that for us, too! We are to be inspired by his model of a sustainable life, just like we are to count him as a model for how to be loving and how to sacrifice. All aspects of his life merit close examination. As followers of Jesus, it makes sense for us to ask . . .

- What did Jesus say about thoughts and emotions?
- How did Jesus handle unwelcome thoughts?

- How did Jesus deal with intense emotions?
- What can we learn from Jesus about pacing ourselves with life rhythms?
- How can we live the fulfilling life that Jesus wants for us?

This is exactly what this book will do. We will learn from Jesus' life all that we can about living life with restored souls, and I'll share anecdotes and wisdom from my experiences as a trainer, psychotherapist, and spiritual director. Clients and directees have been my most profound teachers along the way. They've shown me the most incredible best practices and shared with me their stuck places and their failures. And I have fifty-plus years of life experience to add to the mix as well—the good, the bad, and the ugly. I am no stranger to emotional meltdowns or sleepless nights. I have slimed my family with unreasonable and semimanipulative whining more times than I can count. The concepts in this book have the power to help all of us understand how to avoid burnout and more deeply enjoy our self-care attempts, rest, and vacations. Sharpening the skills introduced here has the potential to make us all more productive, less reactive, and more grounded—in other words, more like Jesus.

If growing in your capacity to handle hard life seasons is important to you, then learning how to manage your inner world hour to hour and day to day is what you need. This framework will set you on a course to restore your soul and be better equipped for whatever may come. You have everything to gain and very little to lose.

Let's do this.

Thoughts just happen.

The thoughts that drop in on you aren't your fault.

You can learn to live well with *all* your thoughts.

By the end of this chapter, you will know *why*.

# CHAPTER TWO

# Living Well
# with Our Thoughts

"Thought happens."

Seeing this bumper sticker on a beat-up Volvo made me laugh as I heaved my overstuffed bag onto my shoulder. I knew that this knockoff of the old saying "s^%# happens" would be lost on most, except for anxiety therapists and those we've treated, but I appreciated the chuckle before a full day of anxious clients.

I looked up at the old brick building as I turned, feeling the familiar pride as I marveled at how I'd come to train at one of the premier anxiety-disorder treatment centers, the Anxiety and Stress Disorders Institute of Maryland. Remembering my initial interview at the institute, my would-be trainer, Carl, came to mind.

"What's your counseling approach?"

"I'm a Jungian; I love dream analysis and shadow work."

"Have you ever wanted to work with anxiety disorders?"

I hesitated. The answer was an unqualified no. I'd been offered an internship at a Christian general-counseling agency the previous day. I'd kept this interview out of courtesy and a bit of curiosity, but the place just seemed so . . . *clinical*. Initially, I'd felt called to pursue counseling to treat people in ministry who might have what I deemed milder, yet deeper and more existential, problems. I wanted to do soul work. I had no idea at the time that treating anxiety would unlock critical keys for healing souls.

"Honestly, no. But the reputation of this place intrigued me."

Carl raised his eyebrows. "Oh, good." He paused, cocking his head to the side, considering me with his gentle eyes. "What we do here is a bit different from the Jungian approach."

I already felt my skeptical self getting defensive. He continued, "What you'll learn here is ACT, acceptance and commitment therapy. The critical difference between Jungian psychotherapy and ACT is what you do with thoughts. With Jung, every thought is considered important, and whatever pops into your head should be taken seriously and analyzed."

I'd never heard it put that way, but I nodded, agreeing. I thought of how deeply I could dive into my own thoughts and explore the depths of them at the drop of a hat. I remembered the afternoon just that week I'd spent sad and brooding, remembering a friendship that had fallen apart. I'd wound up miserable about something that wasn't even presently happening.

Carl continued, "With ACT, we learn to notice our thoughts and then consider whether to delve into them or not. So, if the thought *What if I have brain cancer?* pops in your head, you use the critical ACT question: *Is this thought helpful?* Or *Is it helpful right now?* Then we decide whether to give the thought attention."

Time seemed so slow as I felt my whole being latch onto this concept. I had a dozen thoughts all at once. Among them were: *I don't have to consider my sad and brooding thoughts? What would I do with all my freed-up time? If I did that, wouldn't that mean I'm just a shallow person?* My heart was pounding, and suddenly my mind cleared. I sensed God nudge me, and very clearly and singularly I knew: *Understanding this would change my life.*

While I'm not the type to struggle very much with worry thoughts like *What if I have cancer?*, I am the type to spend inordinate amounts of time on sad thoughts like *Why aren't I more accomplished?* and *What's missing in my life?* and *I wonder what I might be sad about.* I'd experienced the irony of being a counseling student learning to help other people thrive while struggling mightily with my own inner world. I'd become more inwardly focused, but I had no idea what to do with everything I saw. The result was feeling cavernously deep but utterly lost. My inner world felt unordered and chaotic. I had no idea how to deal with my hour-to-hour inner reality. The clarity I had in that moment with Carl was that I urgently needed this new stream of wisdom.

So, no one was more shocked than I when I said no to working at the Christian agency and yes to treating anxiety disorders. I knew that I knew that I knew that I *needed* to learn whatever Carl was willing to teach me. That decision was, indeed, life-changing. I count it among the ten most foundational decisions of my life, right up there with deciding to be a Jesus follower and marrying my husband, Dan.

## Thinking about Thoughts

As I've become passionate about self-care that restores souls, I've come to believe that having better boundaries around our thoughts is a critical piece. In my work I've learned that people are not most deeply discouraged by their circumstances, but rather by their *thoughts* about their circumstances. As I trained with Carl, I began to piece together how my calling to deep soul work aligns with helping clients address the *way* they think. Sean is a perfect example.

> People are not most deeply discouraged by their circumstances, but rather by their *thoughts* about their circumstances.

"I've not been doing well at all."

"Oh, really? Tell me about it."

Sean hangs his head, his forearms dug heavily into his thighs. He blows out a long breath while shaking his head.

"It's work. We're planning a conference that's happening in just a few weeks, and it is *not* going well."

He straightens up and looks at me.

"The backstory is that the lead pastor changed the theme of the conference last week, and before that he insisted we use a venue he prefers to the one we chose."

"Oh no, let me guess . . . you have to change everything after a lot of work."

Sean nods grimly, looking at me squarely.

"Everything. This after I don't know how many hours of unnecessary work after the change of venue. Why he didn't tell us in the beginning that he would insist on his pal's venue, I'll never know. I suppose he likes seeing us collect bids and work our butts off for nothing. And now, changing the theme . . . We already have a speaker prepared for the old one!"

I've heard stories about this pastor for the six months we've been working together. I've never met the man, but I'm grieved by his blatant disregard for the pressure he continually puts on Sean, who is struggling mightily with the ongoing stress that his jarring disruptions, last-minute changes, and unreasonable expectations cause.

"How are you doing inside?"

"Uh, not good! I really need my full focus to handle all the details that need tending to right now, but I keep getting distracted."

"By what?"

He rolls his eyes, then closes them and says, "When he made these changes, he practically dared me to argue. He said, 'Sean, this is how the Holy Spirit works sometimes. I count on you to be able to move with the Spirit and handle changes like this, and I don't want you complaining. You always try to get out of hard things instead of facing your call and all that it entails.' Since then, I've been going over and over what he must be talking about. He thinks I complain? I mean, I have objected to things here and there, but believe me, most of my complaining happens silently. I'm racking my brain to remember every conversation we've had and arguing with him in my mind."

He looks up at me. "The saddest part is how much his words ring in my head. And you know what? They make me question whether I am cut out for this. Am I called to this? Why aren't I more flexible? After all, he's the boss, he's successful, and the conference probably will go great. But I feel so defeated! I don't know why I don't just roll with his changes like other people. Is he right? Am I just unable to handle hard things? I'm so focused on his comment that I can barely get myself together enough to lead a meeting!"

I'm aware that Sean and I could go several directions from here: (1) we could troubleshoot how to get through this crunch time at work, (2) we could explore what makes him susceptible to believing these defeating thoughts, and/or (3) we could work on creating boundaries around the unhelpful thought processes that are making Sean lose precious hours at work. Numbers one and two will likely be part of future conversations, but number three is mission critical!

Sean's inner world is being hijacked by his ruminative thoughts, and while he may not yet value it, my most important work with him will be to help him know how to manage his thoughts hour to hour and day to day during this crunch time so that he can meet deadlines. We can look closely at why his mind sticks to these thoughts later; maybe he'll be ready to consider a job change by then. In the meantime, I roll up my sleeves, and we get to work.

## Jesus and Thoughts

I wish we had an autobiography of Jesus in which he explains what he was thinking in certain situations. Did he get caught up in spinning, anxious, depressive thoughts (like we do)? If his inner world were like ours, would it sound something like this?

- *What if no one comes to listen to me when we get to Capernaum? That would be so embarrassing. Will my disciples think it was worth it to follow me if we don't have a big crowd show up?*

- *Oh my gosh, if this person doesn't stand up and walk when I say to, what will people think? I'm not sure if I should say it. Maybe it's safer to just bless him and move on.*

- *They think I'm a Sabbath breaker. Maybe it wasn't so great that I healed that man's hand on the Sabbath. It wasn't an emergency or anything. I could have done it the next day. Why do I always stir up trouble? Maybe I should just shut up!*

- *Those Pharisees look so angry. What are they going to do next? What was I thinking, telling them off like that? I'm such an idiot, always blurting things out without considering what may happen.*

I don't think this is what Jesus' inner world was like. Why? In the Gospels, he is so very *present*. And being present is the opposite of being caught up in thoughts. Researchers have proven over and over that more content people are less caught up in their thoughts and more focused on the present moment.[1] I believe Jesus *knew how to handle his thoughts so that he could be present*. And I doubt that worry, rumination, or despair characterized his inner world.

## Worry, Rumination, and Despair

We would do well to understand the thoughts that typically pull us out of the present moment.

- **Worry:** A cognitive process that tends to look to the future. It is often repetitive, circular, and unhelpful, increasing our anxiety level. Jesus addresses worrying in Matthew 6 at length, asking this (one of my favorite of Jesus' questions): "Can all your worries add a single moment to your life?" (verse 27).

- **Rumination:** A cognitive process that tends to look to the past. It is often repetitive, circular, and unhelpful, increasing our depression level. In his letter to the Philippians, Paul tells his readers how he wrangles his own mindset: "I focus on this one thing: Forgetting the past and looking forward to what lies ahead, I press on to reach the end of the race" (Philippians 3:13-14).

- **Despair:** A cognitive process that tends to look at the past and future. It is often repetitive, circular, and unhelpful, increasing our depression level. One of my favorite verses about this is 2 Corinthians 1:10: "We have placed our confidence in him, and he will continue to rescue us."

Picture an old-fashioned scale. On one side of the scale is the amount of time spent in the present moment (focusing on the person in front of you, the task you are doing, the physical sensations you are experiencing). On the other side of the scale is the amount of time spent caught up in worry, rumination, or despair—in other words, time spent away from the present moment, caught up in your head. A day when the scale is tipped toward worry, rumination, and despair is a bad day. A morning with the scale tipped in that direction is probably a bad morning, and an hour with the scale tipped that way is a hard hour.

Ultimately, this is a game of percentages. You're trying to increase the percentage of time spent present and attending to your actual life and decrease the percentage of time spent distracted with despairing, ruminative, or anxious thoughts. Success is won with every moment you claim for the "being present" side of the scale. If you have one bad day but have increased your "being present" percentage most of the other days, then over the course of a week you have gained ground and had a better week. If you get lost in a ruminative spin for two hours but catch yourself, apply thought boundaries, and become more present the rest of the day, you will have gained ground and had a better day. If you catch yourself in a depressive spiral after fifteen minutes and pull out of it for the rest of the hour, you have gained ground and had a better hour. The state of your inner world will be improved by every moment gained. Learning to change the scale is some of the best self-care work and is critical for restoring your soul.

I might ask a client as we are working on this concept, "How've you been doing with getting caught up in your thoughts?" My client may say, "I'm catching myself more often, so I'm really present now maybe 50 percent of the time." From there we keep refining the client's plan to work on the skill of being present, along with noticing and pulling out of unhelpful thought spirals.

## Not Your Fault

Our brains generate about six thousand thoughts per day![2] This puts into context the challenge that we face in any given moment to sift through all that is popping into our minds. It's a big one! Add this to our genetic predispositions toward particular thought patterns and you can see that learning to have boundaries around our thoughts is no small feat. Each person's propensity to fall into unhelpful, stuck, and swirling thoughts is dictated by circumstances largely outside their control. I'll talk more about this later, but it can be freeing to know that we are working against complicated forces when we start trying to shift our attention from our thoughts to the present moment. It will be more difficult for some people than others because of the frequency of thoughts dropping in and the intensity of the feeling that they should give those thoughts time and attention. But no matter the starting place, all of us would do well to learn how to shift our attention away from unhelpful thought patterns.

My favorite Dallas Willard quote addresses this challenge. He said, "The ultimate freedom we have as human beings is the power to select what we will allow or require our minds to dwell upon."[3] The fact that the initial anxious or sad thought pops into our head is just the starting place. The thoughts that pop into our heads aren't chosen; neither are we responsible for them. But if we follow up on them, give them time and attention, then all sorts of problems start to unfold.

Clients have been my best teachers in all this. Here's how I see it working: A thought drops in. It could be about anything.

*What if my daughter never makes any friends?*

*This meeting could be the end of my career if I don't nail it.*

*Did that thing I said sound bad?*

*Does my friend think I'm arrogant?*

An anxious whoosh or heavy feeling of dread sweeps through the body when thoughts like these come. When I'm working with a client, we start with noticing the natural, automatic tendency to give those thoughts attention and time. The anxious or heavy feeling in their body makes them try to resolve the thoughts in some way. While this is quite natural, trying to resolve such thoughts winds up making the problem worse.

I'm sitting with Nicola, a young mom. She is biting her lower lip and tearing up as she describes how anxious she feels. I prompt her, "Can you tell me more about what your thoughts are like? Can you describe an anxious time?"

She nods, adjusting her hair, which is clipped on the back of her head.

"It's just torture! When we're at the park, I can't stop imagining the injuries my kids will sustain if they fall off the slide, or slip on the concrete, or twist their ankles jumping off the swing."

At this point, I realize that we need to do two kinds of work. We need to address *the content of her thoughts* (i.e., the possibility

"The ultimate freedom we have as human beings is the power to select what we will allow or require our minds to dwell upon."

DALLAS WILLARD

of injuries) and *the process of her thoughts* (the *way* she thinks). Nicola knows this distinction because we've been working at this for a couple of sessions already.

"Let's start with content, okay?"

She nods, pressing a fallen piece of hair back into her clip.

"Let's follow your thoughts. What if one of your kids sustains an injury at the park? Could you handle that?"

"That's the thing . . . yes! I'm the best person in a crisis. And kids get hurt; it's a natural part of childhood. I *know* this—that's what makes it so crazy!"

"Hey, hey, go easy on yourself! That anxious brain of yours has good intentions. It's just giving you a false alarm. But good work; you know that you and your kids could handle an injury. Am I getting that right?"

"Yes, but I can't seem to convince my brain of it."

As Nicola adjusts her hair again, I can *see* the anxiety at work. Part of me wants to grab the clip and fling it across the room, yelling, "This clip isn't working! Fix your hair some other way!" But the sad reality is that stress hormones are coursing through her body, and the nervous energy is working itself out in her adjusting her hair. It isn't quite long enough to stay in the clip, which gives her something to do with that nervous energy nearly continually. I know it is the work of anxiety, affecting her body. As she reclips yet again, I continue.

"Right. So let's shift now to the *process* work. Let's look at *how* your thoughts are working. A thought pops into your head . . ."

"Yes, *What if Caleb falls off the monkey bars and gets a concussion?*"

"Right. Then what happens?"

"I consider whether to warn him to go slower, or if I should stand under the spot where he's playing. I imagine him crying and how awful that would be. I think of how close the emergency room is and what the best route is from the park. I wonder if I'd take all my kids or if the friend I'm chatting with would take the others back to her house . . . on and on it goes. I'm not even listening when my friend asks me a question!"

"And how do you feel at the end of this thought stream?"

She pushes another stray strand of hair. "Nervous and distracted. A little sick to my stomach."

"Right. The torture of an anxious brain is that it makes you feel very charged when nothing happened *except that you had a thought*. And in this case, a bunch of follow-up thoughts."

"You're so right. Everyone is having a good time except for me."

"First of all, it isn't your fault that the initial disastrous thought pops into your head."

Nicola looks up, and her tears refresh. "I heard this sermon on that verse, 'Do not be anxious about anything,' and the pastor said that if we get anxious about things, we aren't trusting God enough."

Internally, I growl, having heard several similar sermons in my life. My fantasy is to stand up, face the congregation, and reassure all those people with anxious brains that their condition is *not* a sign of faithlessness but rather the product of a broken world. I say, "It makes me so angry that sermons like that leave wonderful people like you thinking that their anxiety is their fault. Your faith is a wonderful *resource* in your struggle with anxiety. Even Paul, in the letter to the Philippians that your pastor quoted, is handling the anxious thoughts of his readers very pastorally and astutely. The 'Do not be anxious' verse comes in the fourth chapter of the letter, after

Paul has talked his audience through their anxious thoughts about his imprisonment. He even says that he wants to send his friend to them so that he himself will '*have less anxiety.*'"[4]

"Really?" Nicola asks.

"Yep. So reading the whole of Philippians puts that verse into context. I believe Paul was a cognitive therapist before his time. What he does in that 'Do not be anxious' verse is help people know how to shift their attention away from the anxious thoughts. But he does it after he has very kindly dealt with the *content* of their anxious thoughts."

Nicola's hair has now abandoned the clip. She's looking off into the distance, taking in what I've said while gently pulling on one strand of hair after another. Suddenly she snaps her gaze back to me.

"I'm going to look at that."

"Good! I hope you will. That verse has been misused as a source of shame for anxious people for far too long."

From there we went back to work on how to spend less time on catastrophic thoughts and more time in the present moment. Instrumental for anyone doing this work is knowing that the thoughts that pop into our brains are not our fault or our responsibility. The freedom and power that Dallas Willard suggested comes in the second *after* a thought occurs. Do we follow it up and consider it for the next five minutes? Thirty minutes? Seven hours? Or do we consider *whether it's helpful* and then choose a course of action? In the "Thoughts: The Essential Skills" chapter, we'll dive into how to do the latter.

Sean, Nicola, and I each fell prey to a different unhelpful cognitive process, and we each suffered as a result. Sean was harsh with himself, Nicola was distracted and anxious, and I was sad and despairing, all because we entertained thoughts that were not helpful to us in the moment. And all of us benefitted from learning to discern unhelp-ful thoughts and then shift our attention away from them. At one time or another, everyone has gotten suckered into long deliberations about a thought that has popped into their head. Focusing attention away from thoughts that don't serve us well is an essential self-care strategy because our thoughts affect how we feel—so much! I can personally attest to this. As I learned to shift my attention, I started to experience life differently.

## The Origins of Thoughts

So, where do these thoughts come from? Are they purely biological? What about psychological? Do they pop up because of our early childhood experiences? Is it about our personalities? Or spiritual warfare? My theory is: All of the above. Because our brains gener-ate so many thoughts every day (remember, it can be as many as six thousand!), we are constantly in an unconscious process of sorting out what is important and what is not, what to pay attention to and what to ignore. *How* each of us sorts that out is influenced by our biology, personality, and history and is amplified by spiritual realities.

Many of us are more anxious due to our inherited biology; we can trace it back through our parents and grandparents. I often say to my clients, "We are descended from the paranoid people. A lot of the more relaxed ones didn't make it." This means that people more biologically prone to be anxious will sort through the six thousand thoughts and tend to pick out the ones alerting them to possible danger. They'll worry, and the process of worrying will affect their mood, making them more anxious and stressed.

Early childhood experiences influence how we sort through the six thousand thoughts per day as well. I'll never forget my parents explaining my father's leukemia to my seven-year-old self. "His blood is sick," they told me. I took this as not terribly bad news. At that young age, in my experience, sick people got well. I thought, *His blood is sick, and it will get well.* It didn't. A year later, at age thirty-six and in the prime of his life as a pastor and leader, he died. For me, this early loss translated into the firm belief that any bad, sad thing can happen. So, when I sort through the six thousand thoughts per day, my brain tends to stick to thoughts of disappointment, loss, and suffering. When it does, I can easily spend an hour pondering what is missing in my life. And this will affect my mood; I'll feel sad.

Many of us have certain types of thoughts stick in our brains because of aspects of our personalities. Ambitious people sort through the six thousand and stick to the thoughts that pertain to their success. Skeptical people get grabbed by the thoughts about the hidden motives of others. People who are exceptionally others-focused notice thoughts about all the people in their world who are suffering and need help. Any of these individuals may spend an hour stuck on the thoughts of their choosing and become nervous, agitated, or overwhelmed.

Anxiety disorders, leukemia, failures, bad people, and human suffering are all products of living in a fallen world. In the world as it ought to be and in the resurrected life I have hope in, no one will have an anxiety disorder, need chemotherapy, or be hungry. But we do have all that here in this life. There is very real evil and suffering that we contend with every day. I believe that there are spiritual forces of evil at work that impact the six thousand thoughts and certainly impact our brains and cause certain thoughts to grab our attention. Paul helps us understand this in his letter to the Ephesians.

> Our struggle is not against flesh and blood, but against the rulers, against the authorities, against the powers of this dark world and against the spiritual forces of evil in the heavenly realms.
>
> EPHESIANS 6:12, NIV

As I get to know my clients and the thoughts that stick in their minds, it is clear to me that so many of these thoughts are not from God; they are influenced by the spiritual forces of evil in this dark world. Thoughts like *I'm worthless* or *I wish I hadn't been born* or *I'm a monster* or *Why bother? Everything will go wrong anyway* or *Any bad or sad thing may happen* may grab our attention and send us into thought spirals that affect our mood—ruining an hour, an afternoon, or a whole day. When my clients are stuck in these kinds of thoughts, the feeling of heaviness, despair, and fear is palpable in the room. I feel the brokenness of the world invading—through brain connections, childhood experiences, personality tendencies, and yes, through evil forces that suggest horrible, scary, shaming, and degrading things to us. I find myself praying silently during many of my sessions, *God, clear the room of all evil!* With my believing clients, we can agree that such thoughts are not from God. And with nearly all my clients, after some work together, we can agree that these thoughts are *not helpful*. My clients' work—and the work of everyone who struggles with worry, rumination, and/or despair—is learning how to get out of these thought patterns more quickly.

## Changing Our Brains

So, here is where our task comes in. *Each of us can affect how long certain thoughts hold our attention.* Study after study has shown that we can change the way our brains work. We cannot stop the thoughts from occurring or from grabbing our initial attention, but *we absolutely can change how long we stay with a thought*. If we practice shifting our attention away from the deeply ingrained, habitual thought pattern, we'll get stuck there less often. And if we practice being in the present moment over and over, we will get better at it. This results in less time caught up in a mood-altering, unhelpful thought pattern and more time in the present moment. After just a couple of sessions, Nicola, the anxious mom, is getting the hang of it.

"I had a big win yesterday," she shares in a session.

"Oh, good; do tell!"

"I woke up really anxious, which normally means the whole day is horrible. But yesterday, instead of getting timid and afraid, I put on my 'kick anxiety's butt' playlist, and . . ."

"Wait, you have a 'kick anxiety's butt' playlist?"

This delights me profoundly. We'd been talking about how to have a more assertive attitude toward her anxiety rather than a cowering one. A playlist fits right into this strategy.

"Yeah, so between my two favorite songs, 'Confident' and 'We Ready' . . ."[5]

I laugh. "Perfect!"

"Yeah, the kids love that one. But anyway, when I was making breakfast to that tune, I realized that my body felt a little better."

"Nice!"

"But even better than that . . . Caleb was climbing up onto the barstool and Maggie was making her own toast, so my mind was pinging big time, like usual . . . *What if Caleb falls and needs stitches?* and *What if Maggie burns herself?* . . . on and on. And I was doing what we've said, but I was doing it with attitude! Internally I'd say something like, *Thanks, anxiety, but I'm not discussing that with you.* And I'd shift my focus to the kids or the song lyrics. When another thought came a minute later, I thought, *I appreciate that, brain! Now back to my life*, like usual . . . but I just felt stronger when I was doing it. It felt like a breakthrough!"

"Nicola, I love hearing this! This is a real win! Instead of spending minutes or hours caught up in those thoughts, you shifted your attention over and over, and that influenced your mood!"

"Oh, definitely. Normally I would have either been constantly coaching the kids with my safety protocols or working out the stitches or the burn in my mind—including the imagined ER visit—until they were finished with the task. Well, no, normally, my mind would keep me going well beyond them finishing the task. Catastrophe after catastrophe would have kept building on itself until I'd nearly be in tears."

As we went on celebrating, I noticed that Nicola's hair was half in, half out of the clip. And she just let it be.

• • ● • •

The best self-care for a sustainable life involves having boundaries around the way we think in any given moment. It means staying as present as possible as much as possible. The better we get at it, the more we can influence moments and hours in our days, which will fundamentally shift how we feel. And this, my friends, is a critical part of restoring our souls. Every small win matters because they add up to make a real difference.

Remember:

- Better moments lead to better hours.
- Better hours lead to better days.
- Better days lead to better weeks.

There is a time and a method for carefully considering the past and the future. In the next chapter, we'll tackle that and learn how to live well with our thoughts.

The way you think
affects the way you feel.

You can learn new skills to
handle thoughts differently.

Jesus wants us to distinguish
his voice from the voices
of anxiety and despair.

By the end of this chapter,
you will know *how*.

# CHAPTER THREE

# Thoughts:
# The Essential Skills

Knowing how to deal with your thoughts
will
change
your
life.
Period.

If we want to practice self-care for our inner worlds, knowing how to deal with thoughts is critically important. Through working with hundreds of individuals and being on my own journey, I have come to believe that nothing affects mental health more.

Being aware of your thoughts, evaluating whether they are helpful, and deciding when and whether to give them attention will have a gigantic impact on how you feel hour to hour and day to day. It takes intention and effort to make these changes, and this chapter can be your road map along the way.

## Boundaries around Thoughts

Most of us do practice some kind of boundaries around our thoughts. Perhaps you can relate to the way it works in me. I wish I were the type of person who likes everyone, but alas, I am not. I was recently in a meeting with a difficult-for-me-to-like person. Paula was leading it in a way I didn't appreciate: letting some people talk for what I considered far too long and diverting the conversation from amazing comments. I was getting irritated and frustrated, and there was just something about her mouth—how tense her lips looked, even pressed in at times. I remembered our painful conversation the previous month, where I'd finally had to ask her to stop repeating her point and acknowledge that we just disagreed. Then I wondered what she was like at home, whether she maneuvered conversations with her family like this. After that, I thought about what a generally irritating person she was otherwise. As I was outlining her negative qualities—she's pushy, doesn't listen well, has no fashion sense, makes jokes I don't get . . . I caught myself. What was I doing? I'd lost track of what was happening in the meeting as I'd let my thoughts run with Paula-bashing. It wasn't easy to stop, though. Paula-bashing, I hate to admit, felt vindicating and good. But as I became aware of just how much of the current discussion I had missed, I stopped. *Not now, Janice. And . . . maybe not ever. Not helpful.* After another moment of resistance, I prayed, *Lord, have mercy. Forgive me and bless Paula; I know you love her. Help me love her too.* Then I turned my attention back to the conversation I'd been missing.

We all catch ourselves and place boundaries around our thoughts at times. In this glaring example, I was motivated to stop my line of thinking because I wanted to know what was going on in the meeting and because I knew it wasn't helpful. It would make me respect Paula less and have an even harder time appreciating her.

So, I stopped. Almost all of us do choose to stop unhelpful lines of thought at times. Say you are about to give a work presentation and suddenly think, *Wouldn't it have been great if I'd thought of having some analysis of the impact of my recent project?* Many of us in that position would follow up that thought with *It's not the time to explore that; I've got to make do with what I've prepared* and move on. Boundaries around thoughts aren't that unusual. Learning how to apply boundaries more generally is an essential self-care skill when it comes to the way you think. The challenge is that with anxious, ruminative, and/or despairing thoughts, we often have different rules from with thoughts we easily recognize as destructive. We often let ourselves dive into these types of thoughts and stay with them, ruining perfectly good hours of our days.

Learning how to develop good thought boundaries is the aim of this chapter. The essential skills are

- becoming more **aware of your thoughts**,
- discerning what is unhelpful about your thinking,
- developing the skill of **shifting your attention** away from unhelpful thoughts and to the present moment using **cognitive defusion**, and
- developing **times of deliberate thinking**—productive processing and productive debriefing—about things you value.

## Skill: Thought Awareness

By reading this chapter and the previous one, I hope that you'll become more aware of the way you think and of what kinds of thoughts grab your attention. The top three unhelpful cognitive processes are worrying, ruminating, and despairing.

1. *Worrier: What if* _____ (insert disaster of the day) *turns out badly?*

   - Worry increases anxiety.
   - It may also present as debating, deliberating, or imagining.

2. *Ruminator: I should (or shouldn't) have* _____ (insert regret of the day).

   - Rumination increases depression.
   - It may also present as brooding, reviewing, or comparing.

3. *Despairer: I'll never* _____ (insert gloom and doom of the day).

   - Despairing increases depression.
   - It may also present as remembering, longing, or predicting.

Worrying, ruminating, and despairing are rarely helpful and are so mood-impacting that we all benefit from clearly understanding how these cognitive practices affect the state of our souls. To practice good self-care in this area, we need to recognize when we are sliding into any of these three thought patterns.

PRACTICE THE SKILL
## Get to Know Your Thoughts

1. *Set an alarm that will go off once every waking hour for one week.*

2. *When the alarm goes off, review the hour.*

   - What kinds of thoughts grabbed your attention?

- For how long?
- What were the circumstances when your thoughts got going?
- Why do you think these thoughts hooked you?

3. *Write down your findings.*

4. *After a week, review.*

- What kinds of thoughts get your attention the most?
- Are you more of a worrier, a ruminator, or a despairer? Or are you some combination of these?
- What resistance to shifting away from these kinds of thinking do you experience?

It may sound excessive to do this every hour for a week. Be encouraged! You'll learn so much. Because we tend to slide into worry, rumination, and/or despair unconsciously and automatically, this kind of persistent interrupting is what it takes to build more awareness. If you are like most people, you have a lot of resistance to limiting your time on certain types of thoughts, much of which is likely unconscious. Analyzing your thought patterns and resistance to change will help you move these habits into your consciousness so that you can make new choices and experience real change.

PRACTICE THE SKILL
## Ministry of the Orange and Purple Pen

One of my mentors[1] taught me this practice, and I have continued to use it over the years. It is one of the most helpful tools I know for sharpening your ability to recognize worry, rumination, and despair and to learn to listen for and know the voice of Jesus.

1. *Gather the tools for this practice: a journal, an orange pen, and a purple pen.* The orange pen is for writing down your worry, rumination, and/or despair. The color of the iconic jumpsuits that prisoners wear, this pen reflects our own imprisonment to unhelpful thoughts. The color of royalty, the purple pen represents our ultimate king, Jesus.

2. *Set a timer for ten minutes. With the orange pen, write down all the worry, rumination, and/or despair that is present for you.* Don't hold back—just let it swirl and roll, no matter how insane it gets. The goal is that by seeing it all on paper in orange, you grow more sensitive to these kinds of thoughts throughout the day. You learn to call them what they are— unhelpful, even downright harmful. When the timer goes off, stop.

3. *Set a timer for ten minutes. With the purple pen, write down what you sense Jesus is saying to you.* This might be hard, but be patient. Purple text may come to you in the form of Scripture verses, song lyrics, memories of affirmations, or just impressions that you sense are from God. It can take practice to grow this ability; stick with it. This time is not meant to be spent rebutting, point by point, the worry, rumination, and/or despair you wrote earlier in the exercise. The things that come up during this time may or may not directly correlate with your orange text. The point is to let God speak to you and to grow in knowing his voice.

John 10:1-18 gives us the image of Jesus as our Good Shepherd. He says repeatedly that the sheep *know his voice*. In fact, the sheep/shepherd relationship is found throughout Scripture, and the sheep's recognition of the shepherd is the way that they have a meaningful and functioning relationship with him. All of us benefit from knowing which thoughts that emerge are worth our time and attention.

PRACTICE THE SKILL
## Discern Which Thoughts Are Unhelpful

1. *Who is inviting you to think?* As we grow more aware of the thought patterns we tend to fall into, the next step is to ask, *Who—or what force—is inviting me to think?* Is it anxiety? Fear? Regret? Depression? Despair? Ephesians 6:12 tells us that the "mighty powers in this dark world" are at work, pulling us out of commission, and that battle largely happens in our minds. What better weapon does the enemy wield than an alarming or depressing thought placed in our brains for us to contend with? Our best discrimination work comes when we can recognize the forces driving our thoughts. If the Holy Spirit invites you to think something, wonderful—by all means, follow up! Or if your grounded self offers an invitation, that is also worthy of your time and attention. But if it isn't God or your wise self, then proceed with caution.

> All of us benefit from knowing which thoughts that emerge are worth our time and attention.

2. *Amount of time spent on a thought.* Often what is unhelpful about the way we think is the amount of time we spend on a given topic or question. Many of us have a talent for turning a ten-minute problem into a ten-hour problem. Our thoughts latch onto something and we rehash the same data, reviewing pros and cons ad nauseum, and imagining possible outcomes in detail dozens of times. This process can take shape in infinite ways. Here are some examples to help you understand how easily we can slide into spending far too long in unhelpful thought processes.

Spending three hours (or thirteen or thirty) reviewing whether you made the right decision about ____ (*fill in the blank with nearly anything—course of action with a difficult relative, enrolling your child in preschool, how you handled the conflict with your neighbor*) is unhelpful. Such a review should take fifteen minutes to one hour, maximum. After that, I would suggest that more harm than good is being done as you spend precious time ruminating. You are being taken out of your life to reevaluate your choices, increasing levels of depression.

Spending three hours (or thirteen or thirty) worrying if the strange pain in the side of your head is a brain tumor is unhelpful. I would suggest that's true even if you *do* have a brain tumor. Considering whether to see a doctor after symptoms have persisted for a while is important, but that shouldn't take very long. And, God forbid, if you do have cancer, learning how to experience *helpful* thinking around the myriad challenges you're facing will be critically important. (More on this later in the chapter.)

3. *Unhelpful timing.* Sometimes you may have a helpful thought that is ill-timed. When I'm talking on the phone with my son, thoughts that may be helpful might pop into my awareness (*I forgot to return that call* or *How can I help my client trust her spouse?*). Those thoughts aren't helpful in the moment because it isn't a good time to deal with them; I'm focusing on my son. Otherwise, they reflect what I value, and I want to spend time responding to them. But for now, I'll shift my attention back to my son because I care for him and want to give him my full attention. The call I forgot to return or pondering how to help my client can wait.

When I'm trying to write, thoughts that pop into my mind about other tasks aren't helpful right then because I'm trying to focus. If I followed up on all the thoughts that occur during dedicated writing times, you would not be reading this book right now. Many of those thoughts needed to be considered, but the timing was off. How often are we sidetracked from important things because we allow ourselves to follow up on every thought that pops into our heads? Choosing the "when" of our thinking is greatly liberating; it empowers us to live fruitfully.

As you grow more familiar with the forces that invite you to think, you'll be less likely to be duped into thinking the same tired thoughts. Other questions and harangues also come into play; awareness is the best self-care for these as well.

## Skill: Attention Training

Training yourself to shift and hold attention is a part of tending your inner world because thoughts so directly affect moods. But your attention also reflects what's important to you, and often values need challenging. One could frame Jesus' entire ministry as a prolonged effort to shift people's attention. From old ways of thinking to new, from the tenets of the law to saving lives, from a storm or lunch to his authority and his words. Jesus was himself attentive and present while calling people to shift their attention to him or to the state of their own hearts.

Jesus' interaction with the crowd when a woman is caught in adultery is an interesting example of this. A woman is dragged into public, presumably out of the very bed where her adultery was taking place. The man is ignored, but the woman can be stoned for her transgression, so the teachers of religious law set a trap for Jesus, hoping he'll say something they can use against him. The woman is put in front of the crowd, so the attention of most people is on her in her disheveled, shamed, and potentially barely clothed state. The religious leaders pose a question to Jesus: "The law of Moses says to stone her. What do you say?" (John 8:5). Jesus bends down and begins writing in the dirt with his finger, drawing everyone's attention to himself and away from the woman—an act of mercy in itself. Then he stands and suggests that whoever is sinless can be the first to cast a stone at the woman. At that point, Jesus shifts listeners' attention from himself to their own hearts, to examine whether they can implement this gruesome and merciless act. Many look inside, see the sin that is there, and leave. Others see that they are outwitted and back down. Then Jesus invites the woman's attention to shift from the dwindling crowd or her own shame to him. He does this by shifting his own attention entirely to her:

> One could frame Jesus' entire ministry as a prolonged effort to shift people's attention.

"Where are your accusers? Didn't even one of them condemn you?"

"No, Lord," she said.

And Jesus said, "Neither do I. Go and sin no more."

JOHN 8:10-11

Jesus is all about attention—in the best way possible. He doesn't want our attention stuck on things that aren't good for us, things that condemn ourselves or others. So let's learn to train our attention on things that bring life and well-being. I believe, with every fiber of my being, that Jesus wants us to learn this critical element of moment-to-moment self-care so that we can be free and fulfilled.

Sean and I worked on this in our sessions as the dreaded conference loomed large in his thoughts.

"I'm going to recite a poem," I announce, "and I want you to listen to my words carefully. Try to bring your full attention to what I'm saying. If your attention drifts at any point, just pull it back."

"Okay."

I recited the poem while Sean listened.

"How was that?"

"Pretty easy. You're right here, and I was able to focus."

"Great. You were able to give most of your attention to me and the poem."

"Yep."

"I'm going to recite the poem again. This time, I want you to give all your attention to the sound of the traffic outside. If your attention drifts at any point, just pull it back."

Sean looks surprised and says, "Oh, okay."

I recited the poem again. Sean stared at the floor, brows furrowed in concentration.

"How was that?" I ask.

"A lot harder. I kept getting pulled to focus on the poem, and traffic was quieter than your voice."

"But could you do it?"

"Yes. I had to really concentrate, but I kept refocusing my attention. There's actually a lot of traffic out there that I hadn't noticed before."

"Right! Shifting our attention regarding thoughts is a lot like this. Certain thoughts at certain times are like the poem, loud and easy to focus on."

Sean nods. It's sinking in. He adds, "Like my 'I'm getting fired' narrative or my 'What did I do wrong?' story."

I nod. "And the activity you're doing while those thoughts occur might be like the traffic noise. It may take effort to keep refocusing on it, but with intention and practice, you can do it. And get better at it."

---

PRACTICE THE SKILL
## Attention Training

The goals of focused attention training for our thoughts are to (1) grow our awareness of shifts in attention and (2) develop the capacity to shift our attention.

Here are a few tangible ways you can practice attention training.

- For those who are musically inclined: Turn on a classical piece. Follow one instrument at a time, keeping your attention on it whether it is playing the melody or not. When you notice your attention drifting, simply invite it back.

- Do the same thing with any kind of music. Follow one instrument, one vocalist or vocal part, or one aspect of the song (say, the phrasing or dynamics).

- Turn on a podcast. For one minute, focus on a noise in the background while it is playing.

- Turn on two podcasts. For one minute, focus on just one of them while both are playing.

The hope is that any of us can return our attention to the present moment, even when "loud" thoughts try to pull us away.

## Skill: Cognitive Defusion

I hung up the phone with the breast center, shocked and scared. My mammogram showed something they wanted to look at more closely. It was Friday afternoon, and they wanted me to come in first thing Monday morning. *Wow*, I thought, *that's fast. How kind that they schedule callbacks so quickly.* My anxious mind followed up with *Or this is really serious. They wouldn't schedule so quickly if it weren't likely to be cancer.* Ohmyohmyohmy. My friends from California were set to arrive for the weekend in just three hours. I'd been looking forward to being with them for months. Now I was certain that the weekend would be ruined for me, as my mind would constantly be pulled into worry, sadness, and cancer-death scenarios.

I sat down to pray, seeking comfort. I rumbled internally with Jesus, and as I did, I felt a nudge. *Janice, what about shifting your attention?* Jesus named the anxiety-treatment skill I taught clients, which took me off guard.

I replied, *That's for my clients . . .*

*No . . .*

*What?*

*That's for you.*

This rattled my brain a bit. I'd worked hard to apply the skill of shifting my attention away from sad thoughts, but typically, I didn't really worry very much. Besides, this was an actual medical thing, not just some random thought . . . I pulled up short. How many of my clients had worry thoughts about "real" things? Many of them. I'd even helped a terminally ill woman put boundaries around her very real fears about her loved ones after her death. I shook my head, marveling at how different it felt to consider applying what I taught clients to do every day.

*Who by worrying can add a single day to their life?*[2]

Jesus' words came to me gently, as an invitation, not a criticism. I realized that whatever the future held, moments, hours, and days spent in worry would not change the outcome. As much as I'd explained this to clients, I'd not yet had to grapple with it so squarely myself. Every moment I could capture that weekend and stay *present* would be a moment well spent. So I resolved to shift my attention by practicing cognitive defusion every time I noticed myself caught up in worry about the callback mammogram. I didn't *need* to think about it any more until I knew whether I had cancer and needed to start planning. As for that weekend, I wanted to enjoy my friends. It was time to take my own coaching to heart and see if it could help me even when I was afraid and anxious. Thankfully, the callback mammogram showed no cancer. I was spared that life challenge at that time, and in the process, I'd expanded my understanding of how helpful cognitive defusion can be.

Steven Hayes, founder of acceptance and commitment therapy, created the concept of cognitive defusion to help his clients get some distance between themselves and their thoughts. Nicola learned it the same way I did, with an illustration I learned from Steven Hayes.

"Give me an example of an anxious thought that's been dropping in on you this week," I request.

Nicola looks up, twirling a stray piece of hair. "This one has been bad this week: *What if Maggie isn't in the same class as her best friend this fall?*"

"Good one. Now join me if you will. The thought drops in: *What if Maggie isn't in the same class as her best friend?* My hand symbolizes the thought."

I place my hand about eight inches in front of my face. "Will you do the same thing with your hand?"

"Sure." Nicola laughs nervously, dropping the stray hair and placing her hand in front of her.

"Now, if you fuse with the thought, you run with it by debating the pros and cons, talking yourself out of the possibility, or imagining the social deviancy to come for Maggie if she isn't in that class with her BFF."

She laughs. "The last one, that's me. That's what I'll be thinking."

"If you imagine all that will go wrong for Maggie if she isn't with her friend, you are fusing with the thought, which looks something like this." I put my hand directly on my face with my fingers spread so that it's hard to see. "Will you do that with me?"

Nicola puts her own hand on her face.

"When we are fused with a thought, what is it like to talk to me?"

"Um, well, I can't see you very well . . ."

"Right, nor I you. We are both more focused on the anxious thought than on each other."

"So true. This is how I live half my life," Nicola said while peeking through her second and third fingers.

I continue, "When we defuse, we put some distance between ourselves and the thought. The essential first step is recognizing that you are having an anxious thought. You start with *noticing* that you are thinking. You might say to yourself, *This is worrying* or *There's an anxious thought.*

As I say this, I pull my hand away from my face about one inch. Nicola mimics me. I continue, "Then I might thank my anxiety, *Thank you, anxiety, for looking out for Maggie.* I move my hand out another inch, Nicola follows suit. "Then I might ask that key question . . ."

Nicola knows this one and jumps in, "Is this helpful? Or . . . is this helpful right now?"

"Yep," I say. We both move our hands out another inch. "Now I can go in a number of directions; we all have to find our voice. For me, I follow up with, *We will be sure to get back to this at another time.* Then I might sing to the tune of 'Happy Birthday,' *When Maggie's a social outcast . . . when Maggie's a social outcast . . .*"

Nicola cringes but follows me as our hands move further and further from our faces until they are resting on our knees.

"Now, my hand here on my lap is what a defused thought is like. It isn't abolished or obliterated, it hasn't been proven true or false, and it hasn't been imagined out to its very end. *It just doesn't have our attention anymore.* It's still there but only in the periphery." I ask, "What is it like to hang out with me now?"

"Better," she responds. "I can see you and pay attention to you, even when anxious thoughts pop into my head."

Nicola came back to following sessions more empowered than I'd ever seen her as she trained her brain to stay present for more and more moments. And my weekend with friends before the callback mammogram? It was really nice! I had to consciously practice cognitive defusion a lot, but I stayed present so much more than I would have without this helpful skill. And Nicola? She started laughing more at the playground as she noticed the kids doing silly things. She was so focused listening to a suffering friend that she teared up! Some months later, Nicola reported,

"My anxiety still harasses me, but now I rarely get caught up in whatever it's inviting me to consider. I can't say how different I feel. It's like I've become a real person. I'm actually involved in my life! Before I always felt like I was half there. My attention was nearly always pulled into my own spinning thoughts. Now, I'm actually *here*."

PRACTICE THE SKILL
## Get Started with Cognitive Defusion

The way cognitive defusion works may be based on personality and temperament.

*For people who are visually oriented*:
- Visualizing your thought in a big, bold font may be helpful.
- Or imagine your thought as a bug splattered on the windshield while driving. Do your best to focus on the road in spite of it being there.[3]

*For people who are auditorily oriented*:
- Imagine your thought being said by your favorite comic or politician.
- Imagine it being said with an amusing accent.
- Sing your thought to a silly tune.

*For those who talk to themselves* (I mean this in the best way possible!):
- Name your brain and dialogue with it. (*Well, Marge, that's pretty creative . . .*)
- Name the type of thought you're having. (*That's an anxious thought.*)

- Name the force inviting you to think. (*Hi, despair. Haven't heard from you in a while.*)

You can also Google "cognitive defusion" for dozens of ideas and metaphors to help you get started. Experiment, and see what works for you.

### Changing Your Brain

Visualize your brain as a tropical jungle. Paths through the jungle represent the way you automatically and habitually think. So, if you are a worrier, the neural pathway for worry is a clear path with no obstructions, not even a vine dangling across it. Cognitive defusion helps you create a new path—but it's initially full of jungle brush. Each time you defuse and return to the present moment, it's as if you whack the brush with a machete one time. You need to defuse many, many times before you have a clear path in a new direction—a new neural pathway. After shifting your attention from your worry pathway to the new "present moment" pathway a few hundred times, you'll feel more at ease with it. Neuroscientists assure us that creating new neural pathways is possible. It just takes intentional practice over time.

Let's be clear: Practicing cognitive defusion doesn't make anxious, ruminative, or despairing thoughts go away. Rather, it trains your brain *not* to take the well-worn worry path but instead to choose the developing pathway of staying present. Over time and with practice, this becomes easier.

When Paul encourages the Philippians not to be anxious, he's not faulting his readers for their anxious thoughts. He seems touched that they're worried for his life and what will become of their band of believers should he die. What Paul does is kindly offer other neural pathways for them to develop. He suggests that the Philippians "fix [their] thoughts on what is true, and honorable, and right, and pure, and lovely, and admirable. Think about things that are excellent and worthy of praise" (Philippians 4:8).

Almost all of us already redirect our thoughts to some extent. I've been guilty of losing my focus in a session, figuring out what to make for dinner or thinking through how to respond to the angry email I just received, but this is rare because I have trained myself to return attention to my client and consider my own matters *at another time.* Undoubtedly, you shift your attention too when you're in a meeting with coworkers or conversing with family members. We're trying to capture that skill and apply it to the quieter moments when your mind more easily slides into worry or rumination.

## Skill: Develop Times of Deliberate Thinking

Sean is agitated. I see him struggling with how much to say when sharing that he's angry with me.

"You can't expect me *not* to think about whether I'm going to lose this job! That's just irresponsible!" Sean's eyes flash for a moment, then he looks down. "I have a family to think about, after all."

Sean and I have been doubling down on cognitive defusion, debriefing a meeting where his boss was outlining his new ideas about deploying the church staff to new assignments. Sean had missed some of what his boss was saying because he was worrying about what he'd do if he got fired.

"Sean, remember to ask who was inviting you to think during that meeting." I said.

"Oh, definitely anxiety," he responded.

"Right, so when anxiety invites you to think . . ."

"Normally I say no, but this feels so important!"

Sean may do well to spend some focused time considering how dire his employment situation is and whether dusting off his résumé makes sense. But what I want him to learn is that anxiety is inviting him to think at an inopportune time and that being able to focus in the meeting is important. He's tempted to worry, but what Sean really needs to do is what I call *productive processing*. That's when Sean may respond to the invitation to think that comes from his grounded self or from God. Productive processing happens best when he's rested, grounded, and ready to give his full attention to his job security. Sean's experience is an example of how we might worry about something in our future and thus could benefit from the skill of productive processing.

Sometimes we might ruminate over something that happened in the past. When that happens, we can benefit from *productive debriefing*. For example, let's say you had a conversation with your teenage son that did not go well. It is incredibly easy to ruminate the better part of a day on it, reviewing what you said, wondering how damaging it was, and replaying different responses. If you do this, you'll only be partially present to whatever the day holds. In this situation, productive debriefing would look like reviewing the conversation when you're rested, grounded, and ready to give it your full attention. In a focused way, you consider what was said that you feel good about and what you regret. You may pray or journal about ways to follow up with your son.

Productive processing and productive debriefing help us grow, plan, listen to God, and ask the bigger questions. The processes are similar. Productive processing contrasts with worry; it means looking ahead and planning for

Productive processing and productive debriefing help us grow, plan, listen to God, and ask the bigger questions.

the future. Productive debriefing contrasts with rumination; it involves looking back evaluatively at something that has already happened.

| PRODUCTIVE PROCESSING/ PRODUCTIVE DEBRIEFING | WORRY/ RUMINATION |
|---|---|
| intentional | automatic, semiconscious |
| grounded and steady | uneasy and shaky |
| productive | repetitive |
| problem-solving | pointless |
| you can come and go from it | you feel compelled to continue |
| involves planning for the future or evaluating an experience | involves feeling riddled with anxiety or with accusation and despair |

PRACTICE THE SKILL
## Productive Processing and Productive Debriefing

Productive processing and productive debriefing are methods for deliberate, focused thinking about things you value at the invitation of God or your grounded self.

1. *Consider what your thoughts have been drawn to lately.* (If you did the awareness exercise earlier, retrieve your thought log and notes.) Where does your mind go when you get preoccupied, pulled out of the present moment?

2. *Evaluate whether this merits more focused attention and energy.* Do you sense the Holy Spirit nudging you about it? Do you, in your more grounded state, value and care about this? If so . . .

3. *Plan a to do some productive processing or productive debriefing about it.* Do this at a time when you will be rested, grounded, and ready to give it your full attention.

4. *Execute!* Your productive processing/debriefing time may look different depending on what you're processing. If you're brainstorming solutions to a problem, it'll look different from if you're making an important decision or doing emotional work (like grieving or understanding your anger or envy). So you might be

- journaling,
- listening to God,
- working on a pros-and-cons list,
- researching options,
- thinking deeply, or
- processing with another person to help unpack your thoughts and get their perspective.

Whatever you are doing during productive processing/debriefing, the goal is for you to get in contact with the wisest part of yourself and with the Holy Spirit, leaning in together about the topic at hand. If you feel anxiety trying to hijack the time, just acknowledge the fear coming up ("feel your feels," which I'll teach you more about in chapter 5) and continue your productive processing/debriefing. You might say to yourself, *Thank you, anxiety, for working so hard to protect me. This situation raises all kinds of fears for me. That's okay; I'm going to keep working on this right now.*

### Better Thinking

Sean decided to have a twice-weekly time to prayerfully consider his scary thought *What if I get fired?* When he let himself think more deeply, without anxiety slinging him around, he discovered that getting fired may not be that bad. He uncovered his abiding unhappiness working with his boss and realized he needed an exit strategy. Deeper consideration of where he wanted to go with his career followed. Over time, Sean decided to apply for a grad program in public policy, a different direction than he'd ever considered. Just days before his first semester began, he told me,

> My wife and I are both excited about this, and I am just so . . . just so relieved and happy. Having those productive processing times forced me to plow through what were just scary thoughts to what was really bothering me. I finally realized that I wanted to shape how things would go and not just be at the whim of someone else's vision. Then I realized that I wanted to shape society if I could. I'm passionate about public health, always have been. I just never let myself consider what moving in that direction might be like.

I think of sessions like this one as the dessert of my work, as they involve lots of grinning and celebrating.

Fifteen years ago, I wouldn't have believed that I had the ability to have the boundaries around my unhelpful thoughts that I do now. I wish I had before-and-after brain scans so I could see the new neural pathways that have grown over time! It awes me that God made our brains with the capacity to heal in this way. And truly, it is healing when you consider that our tired, unhelpful thought processes wind up affecting our souls so profoundly, pulling us away from the rich and satisfying life that God wants for every one of us. Jesus is our model for an attentive and present life, free of much of the internal thought clutter, like worry, rumination, and despair. Our call is to become more and more like him, and I believe our brains are included in this directive. May our brains become more like Jesus'!

We don't always
like our emotions.

We are created by God
to experience emotions—
all of them!

You can learn to live well
with *all* your emotions.

By the end of this chapter,
you will know *why*.

# CHAPTER FOUR

# Living Well
# with Our Emotions

This couples session was *not* going well. As Ken was getting elevated, his tone was shifting from calm to aggravated. "Seriously? You think that telling my mother 'Sorry, not sorry' about being late was appropriate?"

"Well, she was the one who scheduled the outing for Gabby in the middle of nap time!" responded Claudia.

"How could she have known that?"

"Stop yelling!"

"*I'm not yelling—this is just speaking intensely!*" said Ken.

"Now you're yelling *and* lying! You always lie to make yourself look better." Claudia sat back on the couch with a huff, looking triumphant. I could see Ken searching for his next retort. I jumped in, "Wait, wait, wait—let's pause."

They both looked at me, somewhat stunned, as if they'd forgotten I was there. Claudia blushed a little; Ken pressed his clenched fists hard against his legs, exhaling loudly.

"Let's slow this down. Everybody take a breath."

Ken and Claudia were new to me, so it was helpful to see this messy dynamic in real time. When I could see that they both were more settled, I said, "Tell me how your bodies felt before I interrupted."

Ken responded first: "I was hot, and my body was tense, ready to fight."

Claudia followed. "Yeah, I still feel it now, but less so. My heart was pounding, and my breathing was really fast."

"That shows that you'd gotten into a state where your amygdala, the fear center of your brain, was moving into fight, flight, or freeze mode."

Ken offered, "I'm pretty sure it was all fight for us."

"You're right. Once the amygdala is activated like that, it's best to pause. Nothing good will come from continuing. The prefrontal cortex—the part of the brain that helps us have successful relationships—goes offline when the amygdala takes over. Do you feel calmer now?"

They nodded, then Claudia looked at Ken. "You're not a liar. I shouldn't have said that."

Ken took her hand and said, "I was out of line too."

Claudia looked at me. "Why do we do that? I don't mean it when I say things like that to him. I'm just so mad!"

I nodded, remembering how snappy I had gotten with my husband about feeding the dogs that morning.

"The fight response is powerful. If we don't know how to soothe ourselves in an intense conversation, the amygdala takes over and the ensuing fight is scrappy. Some call it an 'amygdala hijack.'"

Ken said, "That hijack is a powerful thing."

"Yes, it is."

The conversation had been constructive up to the point of the hijack. Ken and Claudia had agreed to try to talk about a sensitive topic while both holding on to a value they wanted to work on.

"You two went from a values-driven conversation to an emotions-driven conversation. Did you feel that?"

Claudia lit up. "Yes! I was consciously working on being kind, and I lost sight of that and started fighting to win. Kindness went out the window, and anger took over!"

"You've got it."

Ken spoke up. "So, how do we stop doing this?"

## What Drives Us?

Emotions, pesky emotions. I've had conversations nearly identical to this one with couples and individuals who feel helpless in the face of strong emotions. People swear they'll never lose control again, only to find themselves in the same screaming fit as the previous week. Here's what's hard: It is natural and automatic to respond to our emotions. If we're scared of something, we'll probably avoid it. If we desire something, we'll likely move toward it. If we get angry enough, like Claudia and Ken, we'll probably fight or flee. Being driven by our emotions can be problematic or it can be good, even wonderful.

- *Problematic*: I feel angry, so I yell at my husband and call him a liar.
- *Wonderful*: I feel angry, so I ask for a time-out in the conversation so I can calm down.

- *Problematic*: I feel intimidated, so I don't say anything in the meeting. Later, I regret not saying more.
- *Wonderful*: I feel intimidated, so I challenge myself to participate more in the meeting to make sure my perspective gets heard.

- *Problematic*: I feel anxious, so I don't go to my high school reunion, even though I want to connect with old friends.
- *Wonderful*: I feel anxious, so I ask for prayer before going to my high school reunion and come with a few questions that I can ask so I don't freeze up.

As you can see, when our emotions drive us toward actions that reflect how and who we want to be in the world, it is wonderful. When our emotions drive us away from how and who we want to be in the world, it's problematic.

Let's pause for a moment here. What does this have to do with self-care for a sustainable life? When we live out of alignment with how and who we want to be in the world, we feel *terrible*—defeated, guilty, confused, lost, disappointed, ashamed, and worse! And we wind up out of alignment because of the actions we take when we are driven by emotions that we don't know how to handle. Take Claudia's example:

1. Claudia felt angry.
2. Claudia didn't handle anger well.
3. Claudia accused Ken of lying.
4. Claudia felt terrible.

Friends, I would love it if we'd learn how to handle our strong emotions in the moment (numbers 1 and 2 in Claudia's example) in order to avoid the fallout of harming a relationship and our actions going out of alignment (numbers 3 and 4). Wouldn't that be wonderful? Growing in how we deal with our emotions will, therefore, help us feel better hour to hour and day to day. Better days make for better weeks, and better weeks make for better months. Are you with me? Learning to handle emotions is critical for inner-world self-care that leads to a rich and satisfying life.

## Jesus and Emotions

John 11:35 is a famous verse, one probably quoted more than any other when it comes to Jesus and emotions. "Then Jesus wept," the verse says. But if we look at the broader context of the verse, we see even *more* emotion.

> When Mary arrived and saw Jesus, she fell at his feet and said, "Lord, if only you had been here, my brother would not have died."
>
> When Jesus saw her weeping and saw the other people wailing with her, *a deep anger welled up within him,* and he was *deeply troubled.* "Where have you put him?" he asked them.
>
> They told him, "Lord, come and see." *Then Jesus wept.* The people who were standing nearby said, "See how much he loved him!" But some said, "This man healed a blind man. Couldn't he have kept Lazarus from dying?"
>
> Jesus was *still angry* as he arrived at the tomb, a cave with a stone rolled across its entrance. "Roll the stone aside," Jesus told them.
>
> JOHN 11:32-39 (EMPHASIS ADDED)

In this revealing passage, Jesus experiences deep anger, is deeply troubled, weeps, and is still angry later. There is a lot going on for him internally that we are privy to in John's account. Oh, how I wish I knew exactly what caused all these emotions in Jesus! The commentaries are full of theories, but most important for our learning about self-care for our souls is that Jesus experienced anger, distress, and sorrow but was not overcome by them. Jesus was the epitome of emotional intelligence—aware of his emotions, in control of his emotions, and able to express his emotions.

## Responding versus Reacting

Jesus was the epitome of emotional intelligence— aware of his emotions, in control of his emotions, and able to express his emotions.

Jesus experienced these emotions without flying off the handle or ranting. He deliberately chose his next steps. He *responded* to his emotions rather than unconsciously *reacting* to them.

Jesus *responded*, asking: "Where have you put him?" (verse 34). He was patient, respectful, and intentional.

If Jesus had *reacted*, driven by his anger (as we do sometimes), the Gospel writer might have recorded something very different. Here's one possibility that I can imagine: "'Where did you put him, you idiot?' Jesus screamed as he shoved the nearest wailer in the chest, sending the shocked man stumbling backward."

But no! The account given to us is very different. Jesus *responded* in a way that reflects who and how he wanted to be in the world. We have much to learn from Jesus' response.

1. Jesus felt anger, distress, and sadness.
2. Jesus handled these emotions well!
3. Jesus' interactions were in alignment with who and how he wanted to be in the world.
4. Jesus was congruent. Despite feeling strong emotions, he behaved in alignment with his values.

The goal for all of us is to develop our confidence that we, too, can act and live in a way that reflects who and how we want to be in the world. If we can slow ourselves down and consider our options, we'll be able to intentionally *respond* rather than quickly *react*. And in doing so, we will become more like Jesus. We'll learn more about how to do this in the next chapter.

Now for the tough message: This book will not help you eliminate unpleasant emotions. Handling emotions well doesn't mean eradicating all difficult emotions from your life. Even Jesus didn't get to do that when he lived on earth! But please don't put the book down; there's still more for us to learn about dealing with our emotions. Claudia wishes she could get rid of her anger. It gets her in trouble a lot and is one of the primary reasons her husband suggested couples counseling. But anger isn't the only tricky emotion we'd like to eliminate. What about sadness, jealousy, guilt, and all the euphemisms for anger: frustration, irritation, et cetera? Believers can have added difficulty when certain emotions are deemed incongruent with being a faithful follower of Jesus. We've bought into the belief that difficult emotions just fade quietly into nothingness over time, but that thinking gets us into trouble. So, what do we need to know about emotions?

1. God created us as emotional beings.
2. Emotions don't take very long to experience.
3. Resisting the experience of an emotion requires far more energy than just experiencing it.
4. We do lots of counterproductive things to avoid experiencing emotions.

## God Created Us with the Capacity for Emotions— Even the Unpleasant Ones

God made us with the capacity for the full spectrum of emotions. So, emotions are God's fault. Or gift. Or cruel joke. However you feel about emotions, God has given them to us, and I believe they provide us with wonderful information. And they often pose a serious challenge. But if we can start with the belief that emotions are part of who we are as created beings, then *we don't need to be afraid or ashamed of our emotions.*

In fact, I'll make a similar point with emotions as I do with thoughts: Emotions are morally neutral; it's what we do when they happen that can become problematic. So, there are no negative emotions, just negative reactions to emotions. Therefore, judging or avoiding our emotions, as each of us is sometimes tempted to do, is fruitless.

*Experiencing* our emotions is the best way forward. Learning to do this is giant when you're trying to reimagine self-care. We'll look more at Jesus and emotions later in this chapter, so hold tight.

## Emotions Don't Take Very Long to Experience

It'd been a busy week, and I'd completely forgotten that the neighborhood block party was a potluck. Determined not to miss the chance to connect with neighbors, I grabbed what I had to contribute, which was . . . fresh oranges. I sliced up a few and put them as artfully as possible on a plate, hoping that I could slide them onto the table before anyone noticed they were mine. No such luck. When my husband and I arrived, only six or seven people were there, mingling around the food table, so there was no avoiding everyone identifying me with the orange slices.

"Oh, orange slices! That's refreshing!" a kind neighbor said. I pushed my plate between the colorful and *large* tray of sushi and the delicious-looking seven-layer dip and felt embarrassed. I knew this emotion could ruin the evening for me if I let it, and I didn't want that to happen. Instead, I took a breath and said to myself, *Jesus, here I am, embarrassed.* And I let myself feel it: the hotness in my face and neck and the tightness in my chest. After a moment, I felt myself reset, and I was able to engage and enjoy myself despite my meager offering.

According to neuroscientist Jill Bolte Taylor's research, it takes about ninety seconds to experience an emotion. From the initial thought to the resulting emotion and to the physiological response

74

(including all the noradrenaline dumping into your body and flush-
ing completely through to the point that it is all the way out of
your system) . . . ninety seconds. That's it. She calls this the ninety-
second rule.[1] So, there is a way to get through an emotion, even an
unpleasant one, in about a minute. The problem is that we do all
kinds of things *instead* of practicing the ninety-second rule.

For Demetri, experiencing unpleasant emotions seemed impossible.
He was processing the loss of a longtime friend due to a conflict they
couldn't heal. I could see him fighting to keep the emotion at bay.

"I'm afraid to open up to this sadness."

"What do you fear?" I asked.

He was thoughtful for a moment, then gave an answer that I
hear often: "I'm afraid if I open up to all that sadness, I'll never stop
feeling it."

"Demetri, bear with me. Do you fear that about emotions like
excitement?"

"No, of course not."

"Well, they are both emotions. They don't last forever, but we
don't usually fear the positive ones; we allow ourselves to experience
them. Does knowing that make it less scary?"

He nodded and finally allowed himself to cry.

Emotions have an arc—a beginning, middle, and end—if we
allow each one to run its course without resistance. But that is the
key caveat—*without resistance*. If we don't approve of a particular
emotion, we resist it by employing any method we can.

## Resisting Emotions

I see this resistance in my office all the time when emotions well up in
the natural course of therapy. Some clients are fine with experiencing

sadness during our sessions; some clients are most definitely *not* fine with it. For the "fine" group, when the tears come, they grab the Kleenex and let them flow. After a minute or so, the intensity of the emotion has passed, and they continue to share and process. Typically the emotion peaks, then slowly dissipates. The pain is poignant and has an ease and beauty. I can *feel* that there is movement and shifting as they experience and process their emotions; healing is happening! This, my friends, represents the freedom to experience emotions, which is a key component of a sustainable life.

With the "*not* fine" clients, the session looks different. When tears threaten, talking becomes difficult; they often start swallowing a lot, tensing their faces, even berating themselves. The struggle looks painful and requires a lot of energy. Sometimes I'm able to put them at ease by saying, "Your tears are most welcome here" and assuring them that tears release hormones that help heal, but for some, this only intensifies the fight. In contrast to the "fine" group, this process is uncomfortable for the client and me. The fight against the emotion (rather than the emotion itself) becomes the focus, distracting from the important work the client needs to do. And this, my friends, represents the great struggle that drains and depletes us!

Let's unpack the ways we avoid our less-than-pleasant emotions.

## Strategies We Use to Avoid Experiencing Emotions

1. *Judging oneself for feeling the emotion.* Harsh internal judgment is an automatic response many people have to difficult emotions. *A better person wouldn't feel jealous. No one else is this upset about this. What's my problem? Pull it together!* The inner critic gets busy and keeps going. Interestingly, it can feel safer to run with those critical thoughts than to experience the emotion in

question. My client Sandra does this. Sandra's mother accuses her of not caring because she doesn't call frequently enough. Rather than freely experiencing the hurt from her mother's accusation, she begins scrutinizing her emotional reaction, trying to gauge whether it's a valid response. *If my mother is correct, I shouldn't feel these things*, she reasons. So Sandra dances around in a mental argument for hours, days, weeks, and beyond, trying to decide with certainty whether she is allowed to feel what she feels rather than just feeling it. *Her internal judgment has become her unconscious avoidance strategy.*

2. *Asking why.* Sometimes an emotion may spring up seemingly out of nowhere. Sometimes we're tempted to start processing *why* the emotion came up rather than just experiencing it. Randy, a professional who is interrupted in a meeting by a colleague making a counterargument, may sense himself shutting down, becoming quiet, and feeling utterly defeated. Randy may spin into an internal process that makes it hard for him to participate in the meeting: *Why would they say that to me and not to the last person who spoke? Why do I respond this way; is it because of the way I was raised?* Now, don't get me wrong, these questions have their place. Insight around our reactions can go a long way. But does Randy dive into these questions *after* experiencing the emotion? Or does he dive into his questions to get away from the emotion? The questions can pull him further and further away from the emotion and into a distracted mental tangle. *His "why" processing has become his unconscious avoidance strategy.*

3. *Getting busy.* Some people realize that when they're busy, it's easy to distract themselves from unwelcome emotions. My

friend Beau admits that when something distressing arises, he just ramps up activities that occupy his mind. He tinkers around in his garage, runs errands, tackles a new garden project, and after he's too tired to do more, spends the evening on his phone reading whatever clickbait catches his fancy. Staying busy can often help people tamp down an unwelcome emotion, so the distress remains unprocessed. *His engagement in activities has become his unconscious avoidance strategy.*

4. *Ruminating on the context from which the emotion sprang up.* When an unpleasant emotion arises and catches them off guard, some people resist the emotion by ruminating on the injustice. The teen who feels slighted by his friends leaving him out of a gaming party may feel overlooked and lonely, but he quickly jumps to remembering all the times he's helped them with assignments and given them rides. He spins and spins, pondering how unfair the exclusion is and how long-suffering he has been. *His rumination has become his unconscious avoidance strategy.*

## Another Way: Experiencing Emotions

These unconscious avoidance strategies are alluring because we don't *want* to feel the underlying unwelcome emotion. But these strategies leave us more tired, frustrated, and drained because they require a lot of energy to sustain. Practicing soul-restoring self-care means experiencing emotions rather than avoiding them. What might this look like?

My daughter has learning disabilities and has suffered more than her share of challenges in life. Walking with her through the process of getting her driver's license was one such challenge—a long and trying experience for both of us. One day I had taken her for her third try at passing the written test. She came out of the testing room much too quickly—the test ends when you miss your fourth question—and her face . . . ah, so crestfallen and defeated. I hugged her while I felt my own heart cracking and my indignation growing. I silently prayed, *God, why is everything so hard for her?* As we trudged out to the car, I felt the need to keep perspective about it on the outside while feeling so jumbled and sad on the inside. We went home and had some hot chocolate, but later, I had to go into the office to see clients. When I got to my building, I paused in a deserted stairwell. I had a few minutes; maybe it was okay to cry. I took a deep breath and let myself go deeper into that jumbled, emotional place. I said out loud, "I am so, so sad." That simple admission turned the faucet on. I wept freely in the privacy of that rarely used stairwell, and after a minute or so, the tears were spent.

If I hadn't let myself just feel what I felt about the driver's test, I would have been exerting a great deal of energy through my sessions that evening keeping my sadness at bay, much like clients in the "*not fine*" group. By taking the opportunity to *experience* my sadness rather than suppressing it, I was more focused and present for my clients. We'll go into more detail in the next chapter about how to do this if you find it difficult. In this incident, I was okay with feeling sad. When we have a lot of resistance to our emotional responses, we avoid them. It can become more uncomfortable for us as believers when we deem certain emotions unacceptable for followers of Jesus to feel.

## Jesus and "Forbidden" Emotions

Jesus thought about emotions, taught about emotions, and experienced emotions. As a therapist, I absolutely love this about him. And: I've had to grapple with some of his teaching.

One colleague, June, a self-professed "sort-of Buddhist," liked tackling some of the harder teachings of Christianity. She asked me about a verse from the Sermon on the Mount: "You have heard that our ancestors were told, 'You must not murder. If you commit murder, you are subject to judgment.' But I say, if you are even angry with someone, you are subject to judgment! If you call someone an idiot, you are in danger of being brought before the court" (Matthew 5:21-22).

She leaned in, skeptical as always, but with sincere confusion behind her question. As a therapist, helping clients accept and allow emotions without judging them is something she does every day.

"Is Jesus saying that anger is a sin? Because we would get nowhere in our work with clients saying that!"

I countered, "Well . . . Paul said in Ephesians, 'In your anger do not sin,'[2] implying that one can be angry without sinning. There are many, many times that God gets angry. Jesus, too. Anger itself isn't the problem; the expression of anger can become problematic if done poorly."

Back and forth we went, chewing on the idea that our unchosen, unbidden emotional responses are not the problem Jesus is trying to get at. Let's unpack what Scripture helps us understand about internal and external expressions of emotion.

### Jesus' Teaching about Anger

"But I say, if you are even angry with someone, you are subject to judgment! If you call someone an idiot, you are in danger of being brought before the court" (Matthew 5:22). Calling someone an idiot, or any other disparaging name, involves going beyond *experiencing* anger to *expressing* it and makes us subject to judgment.

Being subject to judgment may also relate to what we do with the anger internally. Are we fantasizing about the slow dismemberment of the person with whom we are angry? I believe Jesus is very interested in what we imagine in response to our feelings. We may have an internal, cognitive expression of anger that makes us subject to judgment. To get clear on this, we must learn the distinction between *experiencing* an emotion and following up an emotion with our imaginative thoughts. It's fine to feel anger, but if we move into fantasizing about the demise of the "idiot" in question or brooding over evidence for their idiocy, Jesus takes issue. We can often make the mistake of believing that the emotion (anger) is the problem Jesus is addressing rather than understanding that the subsequent thoughts (dismemberment of the dreaded person) are his true concern.

We can make a similar conclusion about other dicey emotions, such as lust and jealousy. Those emotions are often unchosen and automatic, part of being human. Feeling them is normal. Allowing yourself to follow through internally with imaginative thoughts, however, is the issue Jesus is addressing. His teaching unveils what is invisible.

### Jesus Models Anger

Jesus models an appropriate external expression of anger, even a quite fiery expression, when he overturns tables in the Temple.

> In the Temple area he saw merchants selling cattle, sheep, and doves for sacrifices; he also saw dealers at tables exchanging foreign money. Jesus made a whip from some ropes and chased them all out of the Temple. He drove out the sheep and cattle, scattered the money changers' coins over the floor, and turned over their tables. Then, going over to the people who sold doves, he told them, "Get these things out of here. Stop turning my Father's house into a marketplace!"
>
> JOHN 2:14-16

This wasn't the first time Jesus had noticed the money changers there. The Temple was in Jerusalem, where Jesus had journeyed his whole life. He'd probably walked past the merchants many times and felt indignant about them doing business there. He'd likely experienced anger, perhaps even expressed it internally, without externally expressing it. When Jesus overturned the tables, he deemed it appropriate to express his anger in a dramatic way that everyone could see. He wasn't out of control, nor was he in a reactive state. We even see that Jesus made a whip from ropes, which implies that he took time for deliberate action beforehand. Jesus models for us how he handled an emotion he had likely long carried.

This story does press us to the edge, however. Jesus' expression is so forceful that it merits some examination. The force of his expression matched the strength of his indignation about misuse of the Temple. Scholars have written volumes about the reasons why Jesus was angry; I'll just mention two here. First, flagrant extortion was happening. The sellers had marked up their prices and were taking advantage of worshipers, who were burdened by the exorbitant prices. Second, the Temple represented the way people from all nations had access to God, and the area where these salespeople had set up shop was meant for Gentile worshipers. Jesus was passionate about preserving this area for its intended purpose![3] By creating such a scene—driving animals out with a whip and clearing the area—he left no doubt in the minds of those who witnessed it: Jesus was serious about people having access to worship.

We have the same options as Jesus when it comes to whether and when we express our emotions. Sometimes it's appropriate for people to see our anger. I think of a person who participates in a protest, or a parent who destroys his teenager's drug paraphernalia.

We have freedom to declare injustices and express anger like Jesus—deliberately and in control.

What kind of internal expression of an emotion is appropriate? Praying for our enemies, even when we're angry, is something Scripture commands us to do. We can also pray for ourselves amid anger, lust, jealousy, or any other difficult emotion. Again, the goal is to know that you have options and to sort through which option most aligns with who and how you want to be in the world in any given moment.

You may be thinking, *Easier said than done!* Frankly, you are correct. But the skills of experiencing and handling emotions and living aligned with who and how you want to be in the world can be learned and improved.

Learning more about emotions
is essential self-care.

You can acquire skills to
handle emotions differently.

Jesus wants us to be
more like him in
dealing with emotions.

By the end of this chapter,
you will know *how*.

# CHAPTER FIVE

# Emotions:
# The Essential Skills

Derek narrowed his eyes at me, irritated. He'd worked hard to figure out which emotion had emerged when the board of his child's private school had voted to end a financial-aid program in the same meeting they approved spending $15,000 on a new school logo.

"Wait, you're saying that I should just *experience* this emotion?"

I nod. "That's what I'm saying."

"Disgust. I should experience disgust? Isn't that one off-limits?"

"Nope. Just like the other emotions."

Derek sat back, then looked up and said, "So you think Jesus is okay with my disgust over the board's decision?"

"Have you talked to Jesus about it?"

Derek considered for a moment before answering, "No. I figured I needed to resolve the disgust before I broached the subject with him."

I nodded, unsurprised. He continued, "I've spent my whole life thinking I'm only supposed to feel polite emotions toward others and that Jesus doesn't want to deal with me if I feel otherwise. Except sadness—I believe Jesus is okay with that."

"Derek, Jesus wants *you*. You as you really are. Not some dusted-off, polished-up version of you. Disgust is what you feel. If you have to wait until you don't have that reaction, then you may never talk to Jesus about it!"

"You're suggesting I experience disgust *and* talk to Jesus about it?"

"Yes, but let's slow down. There are many ways to approach this. Let's discuss the skills involved."

In this chapter, we'll get practical and applicable with the following skills:

- feel your feels,
- reflect on your feels,
- respond versus react, and
- self-soothe.

## Skill: "Feel Your Feels" (with Jesus)

"Feel your feels" is the skill that helps people develop the ability to experience difficult emotions. It begins with awareness that you are having an emotional reaction, even if you are not clear what it is. I recommend three steps: (1) name, (2) allow, and (3) experience.

### Name

First, name the emotion. Consider what you are experiencing in your body and soul, and search for the emotion that most closely matches. An emotions list may be helpful for those of you who are newer to identifying feelings.

Here is a list of feelings and emotions to get you started:

| | | | |
|---|---|---|---|
| afraid | dejected | furious | removed |
| aggravated | delighted | grieved | renewed |
| amazed | disappointed | grouchy | resentful |
| amused | disgusted | grounded | sad |
| angry | dismayed | heartbroken | satisfied |
| anguished | distressed | humiliated | shocked |
| annoyed | disturbed | interested | shut down |
| anxious | eager | invigorated | skeptical |
| apprehensive | ecstatic | irritated | sorrowful |
| ashamed | elated | joyful | stimulated |
| awkward | empty | lethargic | surprised |
| bitter | enraged | lonely | sympathetic |
| bored | entranced | moody | tender |
| bothered | excited | nervous | terrified |
| brave | exhausted | overwhelmed | unhappy |
| calm | exposed | peaceful | unsure |
| capable | fascinated | perplexed | upset |
| concerned | flustered | regretful | weak |
| confused | free | relaxed | weary |
| content | frustrated | relieved | withdrawn |
| cranky | fulfilled | remorseful | worried |

As you identify what you're feeling, you might put your hands over your heart to honor it as the emotional center. Then, name the emotion: "I'm feeling _____" or "I'm feeling _____ and _____" (you may be feeling more than one emotion).

Derek and I had just worked on this. He needed the emotions list to help him with the nuance. It wasn't just anger. He had to sit quietly with the list to find what fit best. When Derek figured out it was disgust, it was as if the arrow hit the target.

"Yes, it's disgust! I'm just sick that they would do this! I feel it down to my bones!"

After this declaration, he started talking himself out of feeling the emotion. "I don't have any right to feel that way. They're all nice people, and they had their reasons . . ."

We noticed how quickly Derek shut down his emotional response by evaluating it. After seeing that, we moved to the next step.

### Allow

For Derek, allowing meant facing the truth of his emotional response and surrendering his resistance to it. When I allow, I might say, *This is my reality right now*, or I might whisper a prayer: *Jesus, here I am, feeling disgust. Lord, have mercy.* This represents my intention not to fight or deny the emotion and my willingness to be authentic. When Derek finally did this, he was facing reality while relating to Jesus, something he had never done with an emotion he deemed "un-Christian."

### Experience

Finally, simply open up to experiencing the emotion. Emotions have an arc: they begin, swell to a stronger point (where we might cry, shake, or tense up), hit a peak, then lessen bit by bit until they end. Often, our bodies receive a chemical benefit from experiencing an emotion. With sadness or frustration that may lead to tears, we shift from the sympathetic to the parasympathetic system, meaning that we move from a stressed state to a more open, relational state *as we allow ourselves to feel!*

I coach clients (and myself!) with this metaphor: Imagine your heart as the emotional center of the body; then picture a ladder leaning up against your heart that leads to a trampoline. When you're uncomfortable with an emotion, envision leaving your heart, climbing the ladder, and jumping on the trampoline, bouncing up to your brain. Most of the avoidance strategies described in the previous chapter employ a thought process that we jump to. As soon as you notice you've done this, gently invite yourself to settle back down into your heart and try letting yourself experience the emotion.

PRACTICE THE SKILL
## Notice Your Emotions

1. *For seven days, set aside a time to notice which emotions are swirling around inside you, especially when you're having a strong reaction to something.*

2. *Practice "feel your feels" (name, allow, experience).*

   • Track the emotions you experience in a journal or a note on your phone.
   • Notice if you employed an avoidance strategy instead of feeling the emotion. Write this down as well.

3. *After seven days, evaluate.*

   • Which emotions come up the most?
   • Do you sense your awareness of your emotions growing?
   • Are you becoming more comfortable with experiencing emotions, even uncomfortable ones?
   • Which avoidance strategies do you tend to use the most? Why? Refer to the list of avoidance strategies described in the previous chapter (pages 76–78).

Seven days of deliberately practicing this skill can strengthen your ability to "feel your feels" in real time, when emotion-inducing situations arise in your life. That's the goal!

One final thing to keep in mind. Experiencing your emotions through a skill like "feel your feels" is a psychologically healthy thing to do, but that doesn't mean that you'll feel wonderful afterward. Experiencing an emotion unhindered helps us return to where we were before the emotion began, whether that state is low or high. In psychology, a mood is an affective state that isn't likely to be quickly affected by external events. Feelings and emotions, on the other hand, are influenced by external stimuli and don't last long. We may feel depressed (a mood state) and then have an experience that initiates sadness or anger (emotions). When we do a good job feeling our feels, we won't necessarily eliminate the mood state. If we don't do well with experiencing our emotions, though, we'll likely make our mood state worse over time. This goes against the automatic reaction of many people, who think, *I'm feeling so bad today that I can't deal with this sadness. I'm going to stuff it.* Living well with your emotions means courageously facing and experiencing them. Remember, it only takes about a minute. And Jesus will meet you there. Only then will you be able to reflect on and learn from your emotions.

## Skill: Reflect on Your Feels

Once you've gotten better at "feel your feels" (naming, allowing, and experiencing your emotions), you'll be in a much better place to reflect on your emotions and grow. It's hard to grow from an emotional experience you deny is there . . . or that you run from, talk yourself out of, or be harsh with yourself about. If nothing else, I hope you learn this from reading this chapter:

- Avoidance is not growth.
- Denial is not growth.

Learning your best method for reflecting on your emotions is key to caring well for your inner world. There are a lot of ways to do this; I'll teach you about three: (1) the starting-place prayer, (2) journaling, and (3) the school of the Psalms.

### The Starting-Place Prayer: "Jesus, what are we going to do with me?"

This is my favorite prayer. It puts me squarely in the center of the tension of my dependence on Jesus to work in me and my own responsibility to do things that foster change and growth.

I prayed this prayer once when I felt that all my friends had forgotten me. I was overly focused on the imbalance of initiations I felt I'd made with friends compared to the number of times they'd been reaching out to me. The evidence was piling up; I was just back from vacation, and it felt like no one had noticed I'd been gone! Along with that, I'd heard that a couple of good friends had gone out to lunch, and I felt stung not to be included. The final straw was when my Wednesday-morning walking partner had forgotten our rhythm while I was on vacation and told me she'd "add our walks back onto her calendar." What?!? Had I become a pariah or something? My emotions took a tumble into a swirling mass of self-pity. I resolved not to reach out to anyone and to see how long it took for anyone to reach out to me.

About four hours into this commitment, I felt the first nudge. *Janice, come to me with this.*

*No way, this is on all of them. I'm not budging!*

I shoved the nudge away hard and fast. But not long after, another nudge came: *Janice, come to me with this.*

*Not this time, Jesus!*

I fought it until the next morning, but something about the new day caused me to relent. Once I had my coffee, journal, and Bible in front of me, I finally decided to feel my feels in that quiet moment.

*Jesus, I'm so hurt . . . Okay, I'm lonely too.*

I let myself go through naming, allowing, and experiencing my hurt and loneliness, then prayed, *Jesus, what are we going to do with me?* and waited for what would come next.

Then the key question came to me: *Jesus, where is all this coming from?* Immediately a series of memories of feeling left out and lonely came to me. I felt some tears as I remembered sitting in a hospital waiting room, waiting for my mother to finish her visit with my father. Leukemia treatment left his immune system so compromised that children weren't allowed to see him. There I was, eight years old, being told to wave at a camera attached to a TV monitor in my father's room. I waved, feeling empty and alone, trying to imagine him seeing me through his screen. My adult self let Jesus meet me in this memory. I pictured Jesus with the young me in that waiting room, giving me a hug while I cried. After a few minutes, I felt as if Jesus had pushed my reset button. He'd comforted me in the deep place that needed it so I could let my friends know that I missed them and felt lonely—and, as needed, admit my hurt. In the end, my prayer of *Jesus, what are we going to do with me?* was met with him ministering to me and me breaking through self-pity to vulnerable action.

PRACTICE THE SKILL
## *"Jesus, what are we going to do with me?"*

1. *Start with the situation that's troubling you, or the emotions that are difficult and seem to keep surfacing.*

2. *Pray, "Jesus, what are we going to do with me?"* Too often, we pray as if the only resource available to us is our own effort. This prayer uses the language of relationship with Jesus and reminds us that (a) we aren't alone, (b) Jesus has a part to play in our emotional reactions to circumstances, and (c) we *need* Jesus working in us for us to grow in insight and toward wholeness.

3. *In a receptive posture, see what arises, and follow the Holy Spirit's lead.* Does a memory come up, like in my experience? If so, let yourself stay in it for a minute. Ask Jesus to show himself to you in the memory. Or maybe a Scripture comes to mind, or a story from Jesus' life. If so, read that Scripture with an open heart. Often when I prayerfully review the experience and my reactions, I'm able to see it differently. This may lead me in one of several directions:
   a. Sometimes I feel convicted of something, so I ask for forgiveness.
   b. Sometimes I have a revelation. Example: *Wow, I actually think I can control my son's behavior, but I can't.* Then I may spend time considering how dependent I am on God for my son's life and for my emotional stability.

4. *Finally, is there an action you feel invited to take from this reflection time?*

## Journaling

My husband's life with God is chronicled in thousands of journal pages. Dan has been known to fill up half a journal on one big decision! The man journals. He writes to get in touch with the deeper layers of his own experience, and he freely explores and experiences his emotions with God. Writing helps him get there. The result? I experience him as grounded, steady. He's a healthy person, both spiritually and emotionally. He consciously fights against the avoidance strategies described in the previous chapter by insisting on being honest with Jesus about his emotions. Because he does this, emotions fester less. Dan deals with them quickly, before a blowup happens. He notices unpleasant things brewing within and tackles them, asking Jesus for help.

Journaling has made Dan a better ministry leader. If he feels nervous before leading a team meeting, he doesn't berate himself or evaluate whether his feeling is valid. He takes his nervousness to Jesus and asks what's important for him to know about the nervousness. Sometimes there isn't really anything more than normal jitters that anyone might have about leading a meeting. But sometimes there is more: Journaling helps Dan figure out that he needs to have a conversation with a team member about their recent negative comment, or he may rethink the agenda based on what arises through consideration. More than once, he's realized that an important voice may not be heard adequately in the meeting and that more people need to be consulted. Dan pays attention to his emotional life, and it makes his ministry healthier than it would be otherwise. He's living better with his emotions by bringing them squarely into the center of his life with God.

Journaling isn't everybody's thing, but for many of us, it's worth trying. The problem many of us have is how daunting a blank page can be. Where does one begin?

## *Journal with Emotions*

I find that journaling prompts can be very beneficial. Here are a few that can help us as we try to reflect on our emotions in a fruitful way.

1. *What difficult emotions are coming up for me the most lately?*

   • What do I make of that?
   • What do I notice about the times these emotions are happening?
   • Are there any themes or patterns?
   • Ask Jesus any questions you have about this.
   • What response feels aligned with how and who I want to be?

2. *What is this current difficult situation raising for me emotionally?*

   • Which emotions make sense to me in this context?
   • Which emotions surprise me in this context?
   • What does Jesus want to say to me about my emotional reaction to this situation?

3. *Which emotions are lacking in my life right now?*

   • What do I make of this?
   • What needs more of my attention?
   • Am I concerned? If so, why?
   • Talk to Jesus about this with a receptive heart.

4. *Write the emotion you are experiencing in the middle of the page.*

   • Use the rest of the page to write the situations that are connected to that emotion.

- Feel free to use lines and circles to make connections and help you process.

### The School of the Psalms

Psalms is the essential playbook for "feel your feels." This part of the Bible completely supports the idea that sharing our emotions with God is expected and accepted! I cannot overstate my gratitude for this book's presence in the Bible because of the permission it gives us to be authentic, raw, and messy with God. Clients like Derek have been more willing to experience difficult emotions after seeing that the writers of the Psalms had difficult emotions too. And these writers brought their emotions to the center of their relationship with God.

> Regular reading of the Psalms leads to a healthier inner world because it models regularly experiencing and processing emotions in relationship with God.

- When I feel lonely and rejected, I love Psalm 142:4: "I look for someone to come and help me, but no one gives me a passing thought! No one will help me; no one cares a bit what happens to me."

- When I wonder if God is still on my side, Psalm 108:11 says what I feel: "Have you rejected us, O God?"

- When I am jealous and questioning, Psalm 73:12-13 captures my experience: "Look at these wicked people—enjoying a life of ease while their riches multiply. Did I keep my heart pure for nothing?"

- When I'm afraid, Psalm 55:4-5 is raw and real: "My heart pounds in my chest. The terror of death assaults me. Fear and trembling overwhelm me, and I can't stop shaking."

These are just a few examples of the way the book of Psalms describes the inner experiences we all relate to so well. *Regular reading of the Psalms leads to a healthier inner world* because it models regularly experiencing and processing emotions in relationship with God. I love that!

---

PRACTICE THE SKILL
## *Let the Psalms School You*

---

Let the Psalms teach you about emotional intelligence and give you permission to experience your difficult emotions in relationship with God. Here's what it could look like.

1. *Plan to read through the Psalms over time* (one per day, three per week, one per week . . . whatever pace feels good to you).

2. *With each psalm, name the emotions that the psalmist seems to be processing.*

3. *Consider how you experience those emotions in your own life.*

4. *Notice whether the psalmist's emotional state changes during the psalm.* If so, how does it change? What seems to help the change come about? Do you connect to this? Why or why not?

## Skill: Respond versus React

Pat was near tears as he described yet another altercation with his son.

"When I realized he hadn't put the LEGO pieces away, I just blew up! I yelled and threw them in the trash can while my son just cried and cried."

Pat's head hung low. His eyes were fixed on his hands as he rhythmically squeezed the fingers of one hand with those of the other. We processed his grief at having let anger drive his actions yet again.

"I'm fed up with myself, but what can I do?"

I asked Pat to consider an experiment. I proposed that he refrain from correcting his son for one week. Instead, I suggested he simply notice his internal reactions when he was tempted to do so. I assured him that a week without being corrected wouldn't make his son a delinquent and that this experiment might offer some insight into his own reactivity. The next week, Pat was all business when he came to his session.

"This was really interesting for me."

"Ooh, exciting. What did you learn?"

"It's anxiety! When my son doesn't listen to me, I think about how if he doesn't learn to behave he might not do well in school. And . . . if that happens, maybe he'll start acting out and get in trouble with the law . . . then go to juvie . . . it just grows and grows!"

"Your anxiety drives your imagination pretty far, huh?"

"Yes, it's nuts!"

"So when you wind up yelling, it might be more about the story in your mind than the present situation."

"Yeah, it starts to feel like an emergency."

"And LEGO pieces on the floor isn't an emergency?"

"No, it really isn't. I mean, I want my son to learn to clean things up without me telling him to twelve times, but no, it isn't an emergency."

Pat and I talked for a while about how to respond with strategies for LEGO cleanup. For Pat, *reacting* had meant yelling and threatening consequences out of sheer desperation. *Responding* meant thinking about the problem when he wasn't anxious about it and creating a strategy that made sense. It also meant being able to calm himself down enough to respond in the moment. That was a bit harder. I circled back.

"Now that you see what drives your reactions, what was it like not to react in the moment?"

"So, so hard! I had to leave the room a couple of times because I could barely stand it."

"But you did that?"

"Yes, I would go into the next room and do a bunch of push-ups to expend that energy. Then I felt like I could come back. But it was hard! I was dying to intervene the whole time."

"Pat, once you resolved not to react, you naturally did the best thing for yourself by going into the other room like that!"

I couldn't be happier when my clients shift from reacting to responding in stressful situations. When we recognize how we're tempted to react, we can choose to respond to our emotions instead. This skill is essential to a sustainable life—and practicing it reflects self-awareness.

PRACTICE THE SKILL
## Strengthen Your Capacity to Respond, Not React

1. *Meditation/centering prayer.* Try engaging in a daily practice of meditation or centering prayer to strengthen the part of the brain with the capacity for mindfulness.[1] These practices grow your ability to become aware of your inner experiences as you perform your normal activities.

2. *Debrief well.* After you have an amygdala hijack, evaluate what happened. This can be a great time to journal.

   • What led up to the hijack? (What was happening? Who was there? What circumstances are worth noting?)

- At what point did your amygdala get triggered? (What made it happen? Why this moment?) Name all the emotions that emerged.
- Did you do anything you regret? If so, how will you seek reparation, and with whom?
- What do you wish you had done that you failed to do?
- Pray, asking Jesus to keep helping you grow.

## Skill: Self-Soothe and Speed Recovery

During an amygdala hijack, your blood pressure increases and your amygdala pumps cortisol and adrenaline into your body. These hormones move you into a fight, flight, or freeze response—that is, into a threat space. When we feel threatened, we do all sorts of relationally unhelpful things. We try to shut people down, change their mind, make them stop talking, threaten consequences, raise our voices, or worse. When our brains and bodies get into this state, "it can take our bodies 10–20 minutes to return to our pre-fight/pre-flight state."[2] If you give your blood pressure time to return to the previous level, you'll be in a better place to respond.

Let's look at how to prevent an amygdala hijack and how to recover from one quickly. Developing these wonderful self-care skills will move you toward emotional health.

PRACTICE THE SKILL
### Slow Down and Self-Soothe

The next time you find yourself in a stressful situation in which anxiety, fear, or anger might drive you into a reaction you'll regret, take these steps:

1. *Pause.* In most cases, whatever is going on doesn't require an immediate reaction. Just let it be for a moment.

2. *Notice your body.* Starting with your body, notice what is happening. (*Wow, I feel really hot* or *My heart is pounding* or *I'm clenching my fists.*)

3. *Notice your emotions.* (*I'm really angry* or *This makes me afraid.*) Allowing yourself to "feel your feels"—and self-soothe when anxiety, fear, or anger threaten to drive you into behaviors you'll regret—is a perfect way to apply this skill.

4. *Notice your thoughts.* (*My thoughts are really racing* or *Wow, I'm really threatened by this* or *I just had a really hateful thought.*) The very act of noticing these things slows down your reactivity and may prevent an amygdala hijack.

5. *Pray.* A breath prayer is a great way to slow yourself down when emotions run high. Example: *Lord Jesus*—inhale—*have mercy*—exhale. (Google "breath prayers" for many more examples.) You could also pray for God to help you remember the other strategies, to align you with your values (like being loving or kind), or to give you a godly perspective. All these are good, slowing interventions when you need to soothe yourself.

6. *Use self-talk to remind yourself of what's true.* Perhaps you think, *This feels like an emergency, but it's okay if it isn't resolved right away*, or simply, *I'm okay; wait it out.* Or maybe you acknowledge, *My emotions are all over the place, but I'm in God's hands* or remind yourself, *I can stay steady in the face of this situation.*

## Speed Recovery after an Amygdala Hijack

When your self-soothing efforts have failed or you've forgotten to try them, you may find yourself in an amygdala hijack. Here are some ideas to help you recover well:

- *Get yourself out of the situation or resolve not to speak or act on your emotions.* When your amygdala has taken over, you run the risk of acting outside your values. You need your rational, relational brain to recuperate to help you choose the harder path.

- *Engage in exercise.* Some people really benefit from doing jumping jacks, tuck jumps, push-ups, or burpees for a minute. Your brain may release dopamine, which can help you regulate.

- *Breathe.* Deep breaths can be very grounding for some people. But they don't work for everyone, so you'll need to experiment. Deep breaths or breathing quickly can increase our carbon dioxide levels, which may induce symptoms that feel like anxiety (light-headedness, dizziness, nausea . . .). Watch for this if you try deep breathing. Paced breathing is better for some people. It can regulate heartrate, which helps your entire system recover from an amygdala hijack. One paced-breathing protocol involves taking six breaths in a minute. Each breath should take about ten seconds (inhale for five, exhale for five, repeat). Research on the efficacy of paced breathing for heartrate variability isn't conclusive, but it's worth the experiment to see if paced breathing works for you.

- *Pray.* Asking God for help remembering what you need to do can be very useful.

- *Try the principle of opposite action.* This skill from dialectical behavior therapy is simply doing the opposite of what you feel compelled to do. If you feel like being aggressive and loud, whisper. If you want to move closer to someone, back up. If you want to be defensive, be open. If you feel like tightening your fists, relax them.

• ● ● ● •

Pat and I worked on nearly all these skills over time. As we concluded our work together, I started with one of my favorite prompts: "Tell me what you're proud of."

Pat looked at me, and I wondered at the relaxed look on his face. He seemed so much more at ease than when he'd started treatment.

"I'm most proud of my improved relationship with my son. We spend a lot less time recovering from fights. He's more relaxed with me, and most of our days are just nice."

Pat was slowing himself down in parenting. He was much more aware of his emotional reactivity and what to do about it. By tending to his emotions, he was caring well for his soul. He was living more aligned with how and who he wanted to be in the world.

## The Payoff

Growing in emotional health is the best way to improve the quality of your relationships. Like Pat, I've seen countless people report dramatic changes in their relationships as they learn to practice the skills in this chapter. Self-soothing is so essential in couples work that one of my

Growing in emotional health is the best way to improve the quality of your relationships.

colleagues insists that her clients take a mini course on it before she will even treat them! While I haven't instituted that idea, I work hard with my clients on their emotions because the way they react to their emotions is what gets them into the most problematic dynamics in their important relationships.

I remember one particularly difficult fight with my daughter when I was driving her home from school. I was working hard on my own self-soothing skills at the time, and I had never been tested as severely as I was during my dear Brenna's adolescence. We were deeply stuck in repeating fight patterns, and I was determined to see that change. I can't remember what the fight was about, but things were escalating fast. I knew that my own amygdala hijack was imminent and that I needed to do whatever it took to self-soothe before I said something I would regret. I pulled over in a rather grand entrance to a private school. The drive wound uphill before me. I parked the car on the side of the drive, announced, "I need a break," got out of the car, and got a little distance away to gather myself. But then Brenna got out of the car too. "Why are you doing this?" she said as she came toward me. I was nowhere near ready to reengage, so I started walking away, saying, "Just give me a minute. I need a break to cool down." Well, Brenna wasn't having it! She followed. I sped up. She sped up. Soon, I was jogging up the winding drive, yelling over my shoulder, "I need a break!" with her following me with a pitiful "Come back!" The short physical exertion quickly helped regulate me, along with the ridiculousness of the situation. An abandoned car, a woman jogging up the hill, her daughter chasing her—it was quite the scene. But what I like about that memory is that it is a cringeworthy reality check for me if I'm ever tempted to think I have this all figured out. This work is hard. And you never know what might send you into emotional spaces that feel really out of control. I'm like you; I want more than anything to be able to love my beloveds very, very well. I want to learn the skills that will help me be able to stay in the car instead of sprinting up a hill out of desperation!

Students of Jesus' life see that he doesn't ruin or strain relationships by flying off the handle. His responses to situations don't lead to emotional overwhelm or destructive behaviors. We become more like Jesus when we're more at ease with our emotions, even the tough ones. When we regularly feel and reflect on our emotions, we enjoy a better way of life. We experience more alignment between how we want to live and who we want to be. This, dear reader, is a vision of self-care in your emotional life. We cannot make difficult emotions disappear. But when we learn to avoid and fight them less, when we are more confident that we can experience them and be okay, we will be more emotionally healthy! Growth is possible, and this type of growth means that you'll feel better hour to hour and day to day, even as you navigate challenging emotions or painful seasons.

Very few of us live with enough
life-sustaining rhythms.

We slide into cultural
expectations of how to live.

You can learn rhythms
that will change the way
you experience life.

By the end of this chapter,
you will know *why*.

# CHAPTER SIX

# Establishing
# Soul-Restoring Rhythms

My son looks over my shoulder. I'm looking at my computer, at the recipe we're hoping to try that night.

"Mom, how can you stand it? You have like thirty tabs open, and it looks like just as many documents!"

"Well . . . it's a system," I say weakly in my defense. I know that my "system" is ridiculous. And I see the computer getting slower and glitchier as I refuse to shut it down in the middle of so many things. But there comes a point when the swirling circle of colors takes so long to resolve that I have no choice. Of course, by then my computer has a hard time stopping. It seems reluctant to let go of any document, spinning and lingering as my patience grows thin—my punishment for keeping the computer going in such a state for so long. Eventually, I get all the documents saved and shut it down. Once on again, it's back to its old self, quick to connect and willing to toggle between my various tabs without disruption. It's as if my computer is thanking me for the break. Too bad it has to run up to its limit before I listen to it!

Today is no exception. While I'm writing a book about human self-care, I'm still guilty of stressing my computer, with twenty-one tabs and nine documents open, plus *Schitt's Creek* in its own window, waiting for me to hit play.

That is exactly how most of us practice self-care. When we're at our wits' end, exhausted, moving slowly, and making mistakes, then most of us are willing to schedule a break or engage in a replenishing activity. But we'd do better to schedule in rhythms of rest *along the way, in our days and weeks*, so we don't wind up like the swirling circle on my screen, stuck and ineffective.

Jesus never seems to get to this point in the Gospels. Amid a busy ministry life, he knew when to work hard and when to slow down. Some of his days were nonstop; others included intentional time to rest; still others seemed slower, like when he and his disciples journeyed somewhere or ate a long meal.

The first chapter of Mark gives us a perfect example of Jesus moving fast and slow within a twenty-four-hour period. If you trace Jesus' activities starting in verse 21, you see that he teaches in the synagogue, delivers a demon-possessed man, goes to Simon and Andrew's home (where he heals Simon's mother-in-law), then heals many people and casts out many demons . . . the last part all *after sunset!* It was a jam-packed day! I would've been exhausted after teaching in the synagogue. But not Jesus: "Before daybreak the next morning, Jesus got up and went out to an isolated place to pray" (Mark 1:35). After all that action, Jesus slows down; he wakes up early to pray.

Jesus doesn't recount to the disciples exactly what happens in that prayer time. But when they come find him, it seems that they expect to continue as they left off the night before. "Everyone is looking for you," they say (verse 37). The healing and deliverance ministry is off to a great start; why not continue? Plenty more people need Jesus' help. But Jesus surprises them with a new direction: "We must go on to other towns as well, and I will preach to them, too. That is why I came" (verse 38). In his prayer time, it seems that Jesus has been affirmed in his call. As appealing as responding to the needs of the sick and demon-possessed people might have been, his sense of purpose is solid. He's willing to disappoint those looking for him and even his own disciples, who may have been excited to continue the work of the previous day. But in this time of prayer, *Jesus has found his no (not staying) and his yes (preaching in other towns).* I imagine that after he tells the disciples what's next, they all pack up and begin walking to the next town. They experience a slow travel day after the action-packed ministry day. And this is what we need to see and internalize: Jesus knew how to expend his effort because his everyday rhythms helped him find the yeses and nos to fulfill his mission.

Jesus models a life of moving fast *and* slow; that liberates us to do the same. What I love in considering modeling our lives around Jesus' daily rhythms is that, while we may be short on some details, his life shows us certain things. Jesus

- moved quickly,
- moved slowly,
- ate with people,
- took time to be alone,
- took time to pray and connect with the Father, and
- took naps.

Jesus models a life of moving fast *and* slow; that liberates us to do the same.

We don't have a cookie-cutter daily recipe from Jesus to follow, but we can emulate these behaviors. To be more like Jesus, we need to learn to flexibly apply rhythms that help us live like him; moving fast and slow while maintaining spiritual, physical, and emotional health. Our souls need this! Our best self-care effort is in creating ongoing daily, weekly, and yearly rhythms.

## Daily Rhythms

*Learning to live your life with better daily rhythms will dramatically change the way you feel inside.*

When Andre arrived for his session, he was holding a cup of coffee in one hand and his phone in the other. His call was wrapping up. "Hey man, I've gotta run, I have a meeting, but write that up and send it to me, will ya? I think we should show those numbers to the board. I'll call you back in an hour."

Andre is one of my spiritual-direction clients. I wonder for a moment how settled he'll be able to get in our time together. But he sits in the teal leather chair that I know he loves. I take my seat, and we both take a deep breath, as if trying to change the energy in the room. We move into a moment of silence, as usual. When Andre looks up, he says, "Something is off. I know I can't keep this up, but I'm afraid of letting up. We've had a lot of funding coming in lately. We have four new initiatives, and I know we need to hire some more people, but every day is so full, I haven't had time to even write a job description. But . . ."

He shakes his head. "What I really don't like is that I'm starting to feel like I'm just running around and not really being led by the Spirit."

I pause, trying to listen to the Spirit myself, and say, "Tell me about a typical day. From the time you wake up."

Andre looks a bit surprised, but he sips his coffee, then begins. "I get up at about 6:00 most days, and I'm at the office by 8:00."

"Wait, I want to hear details. What wakes you up, and what's your routine?"

"My alarm goes off."

"Is your alarm on your phone?"

"Yep, so I check the headlines, my Twitter account, then my email. Usually four or five things that need tending have come in, so I do that."

"In your bed?"

"Or while I'm getting ready. You know, brushing my teeth and making coffee. I try to do that before the kids get up because then we're just off to the races."

Andre goes on to describe a typical morning with small children. They wake up at around 6:45 a.m., and his day is in high gear with meetings, calls, and events.

"When does work end?"

"Well, I pick up the kids from day care at 5:30, so that time is set unless I have an event; in that case, Anita picks them up. We eat around 6:00 or 6:30, then bath time and bedtime end at about 8:00. Then I'm back to work for a while. At least once a week, I have an evening meeting or event, so there's that. But the other nights Anita and I may watch a show . . ."

"And your bedtime routine?"

He looks a little sheepish, but offers, "I brush my teeth while checking and responding to emails. When I get into bed, I mess around on my phone until I fall asleep."

I nod sympathetically. Andre has figured out that his daily routine probably doesn't pass a spiritual director's test.

"I know, you're going to say, 'Keep work at work' . . ."

He trails off, looking hopeless.

"Why don't we sit and do some listening? I'm curious what you might sense from God, having said all that."

Andre nods, and we move into silence. After a moment, he says, "I had a picture of my heart beating fast—really fast. I could feel it. I sensed Jesus' hand coming to my heart and it slowing down."

We both paused. There was so much kindness in the image . . . and slowness. I noticed Andre quickly wiping away a tear that threatened. "But how? I can't slow down. Not right now. We have to move forward while there's all this momentum."

"Hang on before you go there. Can you articulate what you sense Jesus is inviting you to first?"

"To slow down? Wait . . ." Andre let his gaze fall, bit his lip. I could sense him really trying to lean in and listen. I've seen him do this many times. What comes out of his mouth next is always golden. This is the best of how he leads and dreams too. The man can listen to the voice of Jesus. I wait with growing excitement.

"Jesus wants me to let him slow my heart down."

"That's a little different. We can work with that."

"Huh?"

"How about we give your crazy days just a little bit of rhythm that allows for Jesus to do that?"

### Daily Rhythms in Real Life

Then we made three changes that felt doable to Andre:

- We changed the first ten minutes of his morning. Instead of using his phone as an alarm clock and checking email before he was even out of bed, Andre decided to use the alarm on his clock radio. He committed to sitting in the chair in his bedroom for two to five minutes of silence after waking, then getting ready for the day without his phone in hand.

- Andre decided to set an alarm at noon for either a brief midday prayer (he had a nice app for that) or another form of quiet. Basically, we created a five-minute pause in his day.

- Finally, Andre decided to end his day differently. Because he wasn't waking up to his phone alarm, he committed to leaving the phone to charge in another room and ending his day by falling asleep while reading something relaxing.

These changes affected just ten to twenty minutes on tight days and perhaps thirty to thirty-five minutes on days with more margin. And sure, we could have tackled daily exercise, discussed a prayer retreat, or planned a vacation, but I wanted to see Andre first make a change that would have the best ongoing impact on how he felt. I was thrilled that the Holy Spirit led with the image that shaped our strategy. Andre needed to learn how to incorporate his quiet with Jesus into an extremely important crunch time. He started to see that he could have a better rhythm in his days even when so pressed to work long hours.

It may not be as hard as you think to add daily rhythms that make a big difference in the way your body, mind, and soul feel. Too often, overwhelmed people think that the only solution would involve a revolution that feels impossible. Or they punt to more traditional ideas of self-care that involve a hard stop but don't address the ongoing, daily problem. Creating good *daily* rhythms is key to mood regulation. And because these are the rhythms we neglect most often, we fail to understand that *by living better daily rhythms, we can impact how we feel.* Remember, reimagined self-care involves changes to a moment that will mean a better hour. Reimagined self-care in a given hour will mean that your morning or afternoon or evening feels better. Reimagined self-care in a portion of your day can make the whole day feel better. Better days lead to better weeks, even in a busy season.

*Creating good daily rhythms is key to mood regulation.*

## Weekly Rhythms

It was 10:00 on a Friday night. We were wrapping up a wonderful evening with friends when my phone rang. Yehuda, the husband in an Orthodox Jewish couple I was treating, showed on my screen. My eyes widened when I saw his name. The Sabbath had started at sundown that day, and this was well into the night. Observant Orthodox Jews do not use their phones on the Sabbath. I knew Yehuda would never use his then unless something was very, very wrong. I quickly answered. Yehuda was breathless. His wife, Sarah, was having a panic attack, and he had run to the rabbi's house for permission to call me. He wanted me to assess whether Sarah should go to the hospital. Our phone call wound up being all that she needed. We talked through the panic until she felt better. But wow! Could any of us imagine being so boundaried with our phones?

This is just one of many times when Orthodox clients have challenged me with their Sabbath observance. Whenever I read the first few books of the Bible, I'm struck by how often honoring the Sabbath comes up. One could say that God is a bit obsessed with the topic. In nearly every list of to-dos, the Sabbath is included. When the people stray and recommit to God, returning to Sabbath observance is a critical part of validating their return. *Not* observing the Sabbath is written about as if it is some sort of scandal: "My people didn't observe the

Sabbath . . ." *What? Sabbath breakers?? Well, I always knew they were that kind of people . . . What's next? Broomball in the Temple?*

What I'm taking from all this is that keeping the Sabbath is mission critical in God's mind. And: It's part of a healthy weekly rhythm. Figuring out how to make the Sabbath restful has looked different at the various stages of my life. When I was a college student, it meant not studying for a day and trusting that whatever work I could get done in six days would have to be enough. That was rough but a good challenge for me. In my twenties, I remember listening to musicals while quilting on my Sabbath. At that time in my life, I was doing campus ministry, and the satisfaction of completing something on a quilt felt so nice in the midst of the unwieldy and never-ending job of life transformation. With a quilt, you complete a square, then a row . . . There are so many satisfying stopping points! When I had young children, practicing the Sabbath got harder. How could I make the Sabbath feel any different from other days? We had a "Sabbath box" for the kids with toys and activities that they only used on the Sabbath so they seemed special. Now our Sabbath is shaped by rituals; tuna melts for lunch and takeout in the evening. There is almost always a walk outside and time spent reading.

### Weekly Rhythms in Real Life

While writing this book, I felt a strong pull to make sure my Sabbath observance replenished me. I didn't want to write a book on self-care for your inner world while blowing off my own, after all! So I committed to *not* writing on Sundays, and there were times it was hard to stay committed. While working full-time, there aren't a lot of hours to steal away to write! But I heeded the Holy Spirit's nudge and kept to my commitment, and it was *so* good for me. I could feel myself craving the Sabbath when work got intense and relishing it when

Sunday arrived. I had a sense of longing for prayer, rest, and replenishing activities. Having the Sabbath in place served as an anchor and helped me work hard on the other days.

Other things add to my sense of rhythm in a week too. Our small-group gatherings, where I share fellowship and learn with friends; Friday pizza nights, where the whole family winds down while rolling dough; and Saturday mornings, when I write. On Wednesdays I walk with my friend Deb, and my family has tuna melts after church on Sundays . . . These are the weekly rhythms that give structure to my times of effort, connection, play, and rest. My work rhythms are important too. Every Wednesday morning, I do office work and don't see clients. Every Friday, I try to reserve at least two hours for some sort of training or learning. These home and work rhythms give me different hormone injections to keep me in a better state internally. I can feel my body leaning toward some of these rhythms: I crave my walk with Deb; anxiety about my inbox lowers when I remember I can tackle it Wednesday morning. When we go too long without this balance of work and rest, we suffer. Our inner worlds *need* us to do this well!

## Yearly Rhythms

Let's pull back the camera even further. It's helpful to look at the way your life unfolds in seasons of intensity and slowness over the course of twelve months. I cannot begin to tell you about all the conversations I've had with clients about analyzing their busy times within that framework. "The problem," I say, "is when you're in high gear unrelentingly. But having both fast and slow times in a year . . . that's okay!" It's easy for most Christians to understand why we need slowness, but many of us have an intense fear of moving fast. Some people are so afraid of burning out that they refuse to stretch their capacity. Others aren't afraid but have firm work/life boundaries as an act of faith. This topic came up when I was leading a workshop with Christian professionals, most of whom were in their twenties.

Rafaela was describing her busy season, the time between January and April when accountants face a glut of tax preparation and audits. She and her husband made a system for those months: She'd forgo the morning routine with their kids for a quick workout, then be in the office by 7:00 a.m. to fit in a ten- to twelve-hour day.

Jenna, another participant, balked: "They can't make you do that! That's awful."

"That's just what it takes. During busy season I often work Saturday mornings too."

"You shouldn't do that! Put in your eight hours and get out of there. I think you need better boundaries."

Rafaela furrows her brow. "I couldn't keep my job, and I would definitely never make partner with that attitude."

"You have to keep your priorities straight," Jenna retorts. "You'll make partner if that's God's plan."

At this point, I jump in. "Wait, wait . . . a lot of jobs have a busy season. Khalil, you work in student services, right?"

Khalil nods.

"Do you have a busy season?"

He chuckles and says, "Don't even try to get with me from August to mid-September. My whole department is sprinting then. I'm lucky to get even one day off during the ramp-up to move-in and orientation. It's nuts."

I look at Judith, a pastor, and ask, "What about you? Is there a busy season?"

"Christmas and Easter. Contemplative? Um . . . no. More like minimarathons, both of them."

"Someone said they work retail; who was that?"

Tammy speaks up: "I haven't left town for Thanksgiving in five years. I can usually sneak in the T-Day meal, but we work late the day before and Thanksgiving night. And then Black Friday I might get into the store at 4:00 a.m. So. Much. To. Do. We ask everyone to pull long hours before and during our semiannual sale too. But what Jenna said gets to me. Am I doing something bad by working like this?"

It's a good question that gets the group debating boundaries, health, and priorities. A good bit of defensiveness and criticism gets kicked up along the way. Jenna isn't the only one who pushes against the idea of busy seasons; several participants see limiting themselves as an act of faithfulness.

I rein them in. "What if God affirms having boundaries *and* moving fast?"

Everyone speaks at once. I attempt to slow things down. "Can anybody think of a busy season in the Bible?"

For a moment, everyone is stumped. Khalil finally offers, "Well, agrarian cultures like the ancient Hebrews would have harvest times. And it seems like all the cooking in preparation for a lot of those festivals was crazy too."

Tammy fills in. "Passover prep is still crazy hard. My college roommate was an Orthodox Jew, and her whole family had to clean the house until there wasn't a crumb anywhere. Their cars, too. They were all cleaning like mad for weeks."

Judith pipes up, saying, "Jesus had some crazy long days of ministry too. Remember the times big crowds came to him for healing?"

"Right, great examples. A lot of jobs seem to follow those patterns of busy seasons and light seasons, times of stretching one's capacity to the limit followed by times of light work."

Rafaela speaks up again. "One thing I love about being an accountant in my firm is that we slow down in April and May, then all summer everyone gets a half day on Fridays or a three-day weekend every other week."

"Nice. What do people think? Jenna?"

"Is God truly okay with busy seasons?" she asks. "I burned myself out, and I've had to really change things to have a healthy life."

"Those changes are certainly an act of faithfulness," I respond. "I don't doubt that. But having faithful and healthy rhythms may look different for different people. I just don't want people to doubt that they *can* stretch. I want all of you to feel confident that you can have life rhythms and faithful boundaries *and* work really hard sometimes."

"There's nothing wrong with jobs with a busy season, if they also have slow and medium seasons. That seems to be what God sets up for Israel through patterns of festivals, work, and rest. What I consider harmful are jobs that are *always* ramped up. Or jobs that *never* require you to stretch or challenge your capacity."

Peter, a web designer, bravely shares: "I wasn't considered for a promotion I really wanted. My unwillingness to work late might have been an issue. We have huge projects with hard deadlines, and I haven't ever been willing to budge. I thought if God wanted us to do it, then we'd be able to finish it in an eight-hour day."

Our conversation continued along this vein as everyone considered what faithfulness in work might look like.

I have clients on both sides of the spectrum: those who don't slow down and those who won't speed up. Both are afraid, wondering either *What will happen if I let up?* or *What will happen if I speed up?* Having good life rhythms grows our confidence that we can, should, and will do both. Like my computer, we need rhythms of

moving fast and slow, starting and stopping, sprinting and strolling. Rhythms provide structure for
our inner-world self-care. Without rhythms,
we either go fast too long or stay slow so long
that we begin to think fast is bad for us. Fast
is only bad in the absence of slow.

We need rhythms of
moving fast and slow,
starting and stopping,
sprinting and strolling.

### Yearly Rhythms in Real Life

It's fine—even exciting and life-giving—to have
periods of intensity in areas of your life, but you must
also honor your limits. Sometimes this means adjusting or creating
new rhythms that make an intense season doable.

Early in the COVID-19 pandemic, I had a huge challenge man-
aging my caseload. Like most mental health workers, I had several
inquiries a week from people seeking treatment. My two special-
ties, treating anxiety and working with couples, made me a magnet.
Folks were anxious, and marriages were suffering. The challenge was
keeping a reasonable caseload for my own self-care. Telling potential
new clients my schedule was full wasn't a problem, but when former
clients called me, finding themselves off-kilter again from pandemic
stressors, I wanted to treat them! They were my beloved clients, and
we could resume treatment where we'd left off. So, I stretched my
work hours beyond my previous boundary.

This worked out okay; most of my speaking and workshop
engagements had been canceled. As the world shut down, I had
hardly any evening or weekend commitments, so I had true down-
time that I could count on in a way that just wasn't reality in normal
life. Moving "fast" by having more clients worked because there were
slow portions of almost every day. Even the virtual happy hours, game
nights, book clubs, and small-group meetings were shorter because of

everyone's Zoom fatigue. As life started to look more normal, many clients felt better and met with me less often or finished their work with me altogether. So, as evening and weekend activities resumed, my work hours resettled.

Different life situations, different phases of life, and shifting priorities all factor in to how, whether, and when we can push harder at work. The key is keeping some daily and weekly rhythms, no matter how intense the pace.

### Reflecting on Your Existing Yearly Rhythms

Annual rhythms are often predictable. We can plan for the busy times and anticipate the slower times with more leisure opportunities. One of my friends has two kids with December birthdays, so she readies herself for the season of celebrations, knowing that it takes a lot out of her. Another friend, who is a commercial real-estate attorney, has deadlines December 31 and June 30, when she works feverishly to close deals. Ramping up for the start of school is "go time" for many families, as well as sports seasons. We can face these annual gyrations so much better if we know how to be intentional about slowness.

I'm enjoying this life phase where I look forward to the rhythms that break up my intense work life. Every spring, we have a beach weekend with two other families connected to our campus ministry. Every summer, we migrate to my husband's family's lake place for two solid weeks of beauty, water sports, hiking, resting, and seeing family and friends. Twice yearly, I see my very best friend, Susie. In the spring, I visit her home in Durham, North Carolina, and each fall, we travel to New York City together. These rhythms give me so much. My eyes get to take in the beauty of a place different from home, and I get to connect deeply with friends who are so important to me. At the lake, I know I'll have deep sharing on long walks and over dinner and wine with Matt and Amy. Each beach trip, I soak in the sound of the waves on long morning walks. And when I'm with Susie, we tell the long version of everything significant that's happened since last time.

### Creating Rhythms

If you don't have rhythms yet, create them! One of my spiritual directees and I recently discussed creating an annual overnighter with her two close friends who are also raising small kids while in ministry. Another man reflected to me how he'd benefitted from having a quarterly prayer retreat and monthly conversations with a spiritual director. Your plan doesn't have to be expensive! Camping trips, borrowed spaces, migrating to one person's home with friends while the other family members clear out to grandma's house . . . get creative! Setting up the rhythms that renew us takes some reflection and intention. We'll get to that in more detail in the next chapter.

## A Sustainable Life

Most of us aren't living sustainably because we haven't learned how to apply life-giving rhythms that help restore our souls. With the pressures and expectations of our society, we're becoming less and less likely to do daily, weekly, and yearly rhythms well *without intentional effort*. The fact that we can affect our rhythms isn't known and utilized enough! In my therapy practice, I talk to people about these concepts nearly every day. Momentum carries most of us toward the fast end of the spectrum, and we tend to stay there too long. People who wake up to that reality are inclined to overcorrect, either refusing to have fast seasons or conceptualizing them as inherently bad.

With appropriate rhythms applied to the various seasons of your life, your soul can thrive, even when certain roles require more of you. Remember, Jesus came to give you a rich and satisfying life! Finding the right rhythms for the right time is how you get closer to that life.

Let's learn how to do this.

The best self-care involves
soul-restoring rhythms.

You can learn to create
better rhythms in your life.

God created us with this need
and wants this for us.

By the end of this chapter,
you will know *how*.

# CHAPTER SEVEN

# Rhythms:
# The Essential Skills

My housemate, Char, had cooked that evening—tortilla soup! The smell had been filling the house, and we were all eager to eat. The first bite surprised: It had quite a kick but was still tasty. Second bite, the kick seemed a bit overpowering. By the fourth and fifth bites, none of us could taste anything except the fire blazing in our mouths. We looked at each other helplessly. Char conceded, "This can't be right. I'm dying here!"

A look at the recipe revealed the problem: Char had added one table-spoon of cayenne pepper instead of one teaspoon. It was a good soup at the core; it just had too much cayenne for our unaccustomed mouths.

## Hormone Soup

Think of your body as a kind of hormone soup. A large amount of stress hormones, and the soup is too spicy. Not enough spice, and the soup is flavorless. We need stress hormones, but having too large a quantity of them too consistently can make for a horrible-tasting soup. In our bodies, this means feeling anxious and stressed. We need to make sure we're adding other seasonings throughout the day. We do this by getting boosts of happy hormones, like dopamine and oxytocin. This can happen through things like connecting with God or people, moving our bodies, or taking good breaks. If we don't have all these things happening in most of our days, we'll likely have a spicy soup. I would love for every person who reads this book to become a better chef for the soup that is being cooked every day in their bodies. And learning how to make better hormone soup is the goal of this chapter. Just like Char's soup was ruined by the extra cayenne, your body's hormone soup can be thrown off balance by too large a quantity of stress hormones.

But here's where common messages about self-care—like "De-stress!" or "Eliminate stressors!" or simply "Calm down."—come up short. These messages lead us to a quandary. Sometimes we can't simply get rid of the stressors in our lives. It's no simple choice to quit our demanding job or stop parenting our troubled child or just quit our intense cancer treatment. Some stressors aren't eliminable! The mandate to get rid of stress can land us in a puddle of self-defeat.

Eliminating stress isn't the only option. Potatoes soak up spices and can mellow the intensity of an overspiced soup. Adding brown sugar is also a secret of chefs for calming spicy soups. We have similar options with our hormone soup: things we can add to our lives, rhythms that can really make a difference when we have a lot of stress hormones in our bodies. Find the potatoes and brown sugar that you really like and that you'll *want* to add to your life! This is the critical inner-world work that will keep you thriving during busy times. And I'd be remiss if I didn't say that some meassure of stress hormones is desirable. Soup with no cayenne (or the like) is bland. Without the zest that stress and stress hormones can add, our lives can taste similarly boring.

## A Hard Truth

Stress hormones aren't evenly distributed, and it isn't fair. People experiencing poverty have more stress hormones day to day and hour to hour than people who don't. People experiencing systemic racism have more stress hormones day to day, hour to hour than those who don't. Bodies suffer this injustice with all the signs of chronic stress-hormone imbalance, including increased risk of many physical illnesses as well as mental health challenges. For others, the injustice of a stress imbalance is temporary yet still fundamentally unfair: an illness hits, or a business takes a financial blow, or a child rebels. In these times, our bodies are flooded with stress hormones, putting us in a chronically imbalanced state. Still others are genetically predisposed to anxiety or depression, thus making their stress-hormone levels higher overall. It isn't fair. The stock that we're starting our soup with isn't the same. But the methods for making better soup apply to all of us.

So, whatever the starting place, the treatment is the same: Get a better balance of hormones in your body. We do this by addressing our life rhythms as well as we can. I tell my clients that they really can *do something* about their own situations—even if we can't immediately change society, the situation, or the genes, *we can make better hormone soup.* And I believe Jesus wants that for us as a small step toward righting the unfair distribution of stress hormones in this world.

> Even if we can't immediately change society, the situation, or the genes, we can make better hormone soup.

Let's get into the ingredients and start creating a recipe for tasty soup.

## Know Your Hormones

*Adrenaline and cortisol.* These hormones are triggered by stress. They may flood our bodies during a life-threatening event. But they may also activate when we get a demanding work email, our spouse yells at us, our kids' behavior freaks us out, we get an alarming text, or we see a disturbing headline. We also get these hormones at very helpful times: when facing a deadline, anticipating a big presentation, having an important talk with our teenager, or engaging in a vulnerable conversation with a beloved friend. Stress hormones pump us up and give us some oomph when we need it.

The problem with these hormones isn't that we have them—we need them! The problem is when we have chronic, high levels of adrenaline and cortisol without rhythms that provide adequate influxes of other hormones, both in the short and long terms: daily rhythms and breaks *and* broader rhythms and breaks like weekends, Sabbaths, vacations, fun activities, and connection points with people. Without good rhythms to provide these other hormones, the stress hormones run amok, potentially causing problems with weight, sleep, heart health, mood regulation, and/or concentration.

The thing is: If we have good life rhythms, *we can affect*, to a degree, the amount of stress hormones in our bodies at any time. Knowing how to practice good rhythms can give us an amazing lift. Yes, in any given hour, day, or week.

*Dopamine and endorphins.* These are the "happy hormones" that impact the brain's reward system. Dopamine helps us feel good! In any given day, we can increase our dopamine levels by getting adequate sleep and exercise; listening to music; praying, meditating, and worshiping; eating protein or dark chocolate; and limiting our saturated-fat intake. Endorphins help us deal with pain and enhance pleasure. We get these through activities that make us feel good, with exercise at the top of the list. A runner's high is an experience of endorphins in the body.

*Oxytocin.* Famously known as the "love hormone," oxytocin comes when hugging or cuddling (in either a sexual or a nonsexual way). Oxytocin also comes through nonphysical connection—texting, talking, coffee or dinner, and FaceTime or phone calls all count. Connecting with Jesus counts too: We can get an influx of oxytocin from praying or worshiping.

These hormones, when in balance with stress hormones, make for a well-seasoned hormone soup. What that feels like in day-to-day living is steadiness in your inner world. You want a mix of stress hormones and happy hormones at any time, and *you can influence this if you are intentional.*

## Jesus as Our Example

Jesus modeled a life of flexible rhythms, which makes him a squirrelly model for having daily rhythms. He didn't do the same thing every day, yet he led a balanced life. Just look at Jesus' prayer times. We read of times that he prayed in the morning, but we don't know if he did that every day. Now, that is *not* the message I got in my college fellowship! We were told we needed a "quiet time," and it had to be in the morning or your efforts were second-class. Jesus also went away to a lonely place to pray at points, but he was okay with being interrupted. In the Gospel of Luke, he prays *after* doing ministry. So, Jesus' prayer life varied according to the situation.

In our own rhythms, there are many ways to incorporate prayer on a regular basis. It doesn't have to be a cookie-cutter model in the name of "living like Jesus did." Jesus models flexibility and a deep commitment to being connected to God, and he accomplished this in various ways. I love this because it gives us freedom to find a prayer life that suits us and our life circumstances. By looking at the concepts of better breaks, better mornings, and better bedtimes, we'll see the many ways that prayer—along with other hormone-helpful activities—can be a built-in practice that helps you live better during stressful times.

## Skill: Better Breaks

Bella, a student in film school, was complaining about becoming less focused and more anxiety driven and stressed. As a woman of color, the pressure she felt to succeed was intense, and we'd discussed how she felt she had to outperform everyone simply to stay in good standing. We'd just reviewed the idea of hormone soup again, and we were examining her days working on film projects.

I asked, "Do you take breaks during the day?"

"Yeah, I'm really good about that," Bella replied.

"And what do you do during your break?"

"I love tea, so I usually make a cup."

"Great! And do you actually stop editing while you drink it?"

"A little, while I check social media, you know. Just to turn off my brain for a bit."

"Does that turn off your brain?"

"Well, no . . . it's different from work, though. Except . . ."

I lean in, interested in what she might say next.

"Mostly it sucks me in and I forget about work. But my brain?

Social media usually revs it up. A headline makes me mad, or a post makes me worried I missed something fun."

Bella flips her phone over and over in her hand as she talks to me. She looks down at it and seems to suddenly notice the irony.

"Honestly, I don't know what I'd do for a break besides mess around on my phone. What do other people do?"

"Most people do exactly what you do, including me. To do anything otherwise, I have to be really intentional. And hey, there's nothing inherently wrong with messing around on your phone during a break! But if you're feeling as bad as you are these days, overstimulated and unfocused, it bears reconsidering. I'm saying take some of that time for a *better* break. One that slows your brain down rather than revving it up."

"For my hormone soup . . . right, Chef?"

Bella's eyebrows are raised as she eyes me mischievously, having mocked my metaphor more than a few times.

This simple concept entails taking a break that gives your brain and body a *different* experience from that of a typical busy workday. There are many ways to do it. My favorite is having a mindful bit of chocolate. I get a few peanut M&M's and eat them slowly, *without doing anything else.* I endeavor to keep my attention on the taste of the chocolate as it melts, the crunch of the peanut, the sweet and salty mix of flavors . . . Just doing this for three to four minutes changes the energy and rhythm of my brain and therefore my body because I'm adding a pinch of new hormone to the soup. I really love peanut M&M's, so my dopamine hit is high for this mindful break!

A better break is easy enough to take, but I don't know *anyone* who automatically does it. Intentionality is required, so set an alarm or write yourself a sticky note.

Better breaks lead to better hours, which affect days, remember? So, be intentional!

---

### Start Taking Better Breaks

1. *Consider your typical day as it is currently.*

   - Do you take breaks? If so, what are they like? Is there potential for them to become better?
   - If you don't take breaks, consider when a break could fit in and decide your strategy. Set a calendar reminder or write "take break" on a note to make sure this isn't forgotten.

2. *What could a better break that suits you look like?* Consider the following ideas, or come up with a few of your own.

   - having a mindful hot chocolate, or a mindful clementine, or a mindful mint
   - walking around the block or office just to move your body
   - reading something spiritually encouraging or uplifting
   - doing some stretches that help release tight muscles
   - listening to the Holy Spirit, like Andre in the previous chapter
   - listening to a song
   - praying the hours[1] or doing a morning, midday, or evening liturgy
   - checking in with a friend or colleague

3. *After a two-week period, review.*

- What are you noticing? Do you like your better breaks? Do you sense an immediate benefit to taking them? How about a more overall benefit? Remember, we're going for a flavor change in your soup!
- Do you want to try other kinds of better breaks at this point? Or add more better breaks?
- Set your intention, and review again in two weeks.

Bella committed to this and discovered that she loved taking her tea to a window that overlooked a courtyard with trees. From her vantage point on the third floor, she could see into the canopy, and she spent her tea breaks watching the branches stir in the breeze. Often it became a moment of prayerful gratitude. Bella could feel the impact of letting her brain settle into a different speed for those times. One day, she explains, "My tea-tree breaks also seem to help me out of creative stuck places. After a break, I'm in a more focused place. I have fresh eyes to see my project, and some of my best breakthroughs come after I've taken one. So thanks, Chef!"

We laugh, and I marvel at how better hormone soup turns so many things around.

## Skill: Better Mornings/Bedtimes

I've vowed not to do too much "back in the day . . ." talking in this book, but some of you may remember a time when we had to put on a bathrobe, walk outside, pick up a newspaper, and open it before our brains got jarred into action. We had a natural transition time of at least a few minutes before the outside world came crashing in. No longer. Most of us have seen headlines and checked work email before visiting the bathroom in the morning.

Quite simply, a better morning allows your brain, and therefore your body, to wake up more gently and slowly. Like soup a chef starts with homemade stock, your hormone soup can be greatly helped by a better morning rhythm. For this reason, many of my clients have switched back to using alarm clocks so the pull of headlines, texts, and social media isn't in the room when they wake. Other people put their phones on airplane mode until a designated time. Phone hygiene is step one for most of us who want a better morning, but what does easing into the day mean for you?

The same principle holds for bedtime: Your brain needs time to power down slowly. Rather than ramping up your brain and body with a final check of email before bed, move yourself toward sleep like you might a toddler. Our needs are just like theirs! We need help to learn how to do bedtime well.

PRACTICE THE SKILL
## A Better Morning/Better Bedtime

What makes a great morning/bedtime to you? Here are some practices you could try as part of a slower start in the morning or a gentler power-down at bedtime. Beginning and ending your days well will keep your hormone soup fresh and tasty.

*Better morning practices:*
- delay checking your phone (perhaps by keeping it turned off or putting it on airplane mode)
- pray
- journal
- read Scripture
- drink coffee

- eat a nutritious breakfast
- exercise
- spend time outdoors
- read the news
- prep for your day
- connect with your spouse/housemates/children
- enjoy silence
- listen to music
- do yoga
- meditate

*Better bedtime practices:*
- turn off your phone well before bedtime
- end screen time one to two hours before bed
- refrain from checking email or social media after a certain time
- pray
- read Scripture
- do the evening Examen[2] and/or Compline[3]
- journal
- read (without blue light)
- do a day-ending ritual (turn off lights, lock doors, etc.)
- engage in a nighttime hygiene routine (wash face, brush teeth, etc.)
- connect with your spouse or housemates
- have a good-night phone call with someone
- enjoy silence
- listen to music
- play a sound machine
- do yoga
- meditate

Most of us can't do all the things that make a morning/bedtime ideal every day, but which of these ideas appeal to you most?

1. *Plan.* Even if we're busy, it may be possible to incorporate two to four of the components of an ideal morning or bedtime into our days. Once you've chosen two to four practices that might work well for you, come up with a specific plan. For example, what exactly would you listen to or read? If you plan to journal, do you have a notebook already? Get prepared.

2. *Implement.* Commit to experimenting with these two to four practices for two weeks. Feel free to adjust which practices you do as you see fit.

3. *Evaluate.* After two weeks, consider how it's going. What do you notice about the way your morning/bedtime feels different with these practices? What do you notice about your days when you have a better morning/bedtime?

4. *Retool.* What adjustments do you need to make from here? Would you like to add another component to your morning/bedtime? Would you like to try another of the suggested practices or come up with one of your own?

After slowly becoming convinced of not only taking better breaks but also having better mornings and bedtimes, Bella reported this in therapy. "I've been off my anxiety medication for three months now, and I really feel okay. I never thought that would happen."

"What do you like about your life with these adjustments?" I ask.

"Adopting these new routines has been a spiritual challenge. Slowing down for better breaks, mornings, and bedtimes requires trusting Jesus with my future. The drive to work nonstop comes from fear that I won't make it, that whatever project I'm working on won't get the grade or win the award. I have to say a prayer to even have the courage to slow down! Otherwise, fear drives me. Before we worked on this, I didn't see how afraid I was. The surprise for me in making these changes is that I feel closer to Jesus. Better breaks, mornings, and bedtimes are moments of surrender and trust. Plus, I just feel better when I take care of myself this way. So, Chef, I suppose I've become a chef myself."

So many people are like Bella, giving up on making any changes because they've bought into the idea that the only thing that can help is something they can't fathom doing, like quitting their job. Bella became much happier and more effective by establishing small—yet significant—daily rhythms. Better breaks, mornings, and bedtimes: yet another way that changing a few moments can change an hour, which affects a day . . . et cetera. You can do this!

## Skill: Better Sleep

Psalm 4:8 encourages me: "In peace I will lie down and sleep, for you alone, O Lord, will keep me safe."

Sleep is fundamentally an act of trust, and it's a big deal in our inner-world self-care. To get the sleep we need, we must be willing to admit that the day's work is done. We surrender our tasks and concerns to God. Waking and sleeping are the most elemental rhythms we need to be regulated. When sleep rhythms are off balance, we become irritable and emotionally fragile, and we lose our emotional and mental resilience. I've made a rule for myself: If I don't sleep well one night, I just carry on and have the best day possible. But if I don't sleep well two or three nights, I refrain from all big-picture questions or existential musings. Without quality sleep, my perspective becomes so bleak and hopeless that entertaining such ponderings goes nowhere, *fast.*

The importance of sleep is a firm reality, so much so that I normally ask clients about sleep in our first session. A handful of clients have only needed two or three sessions because once the sleep issue is resolved, their other symptoms disappear. Sleep is that important. If your sleep rhythms aren't great, I strongly encourage you to tackle this skill.

PRACTICE THE SKILL
## Get Better Sleep

Following a few sleep principles can make a big difference in your well-being. Some of these overlap with the "better bedtime practices" already described, but they bear repeating because of their importance.

- *Stop screen usage one to two hours before bedtime.* This practice helps your brain be less stimulated, so sleep will come more easily. If you must use a digital device just before going to bed, apply a blue-light filter.

- *Create a routine that cues your body, mind, and soul that it is bedtime.* For ideas, see the section on better bedtime practices.

- You need to be awake for fourteen to sixteen hours before trying to sleep at night. So, if you sleep until 11:00 a.m. and can't sleep the following night at 10:00 p.m., don't diagnose yourself as a night owl too quickly. *To achieve your desired bedtime, you may need to adjust your waking time.*

- Similarly, although naps are great and have their place, long ones can disrupt nighttime sleep. *If you're trying to regulate your sleep, consider your nap schedule.*

- *Never stay in bed awake for more than about twenty to thirty minutes.* (We quickly habituate to being in bed awake.) If you're having trouble sleeping, try reading in a comfy chair for a while. Don't go back to bed until you're tired.

- *Follow the same pattern when you're feeling anxious.* (We can also train ourselves to worry in bed.) Get up to read, then try sleeping again once the anxiety subsides.

- *Stop drinking water two to three hours before bedtime.*[4] This can help you sleep through the night without being interrupted by bathroom visits.

- *Experiment with other sleep-helping changes.* Here are a few my clients have made: adding blackout curtains or a sound machine, changing pet sleep configuration and/or access, getting a new mattress, and trying a different bedroom temperature.

Think about which of these practices might help improve your sleep quality. Add one or two of these practices into your life for two weeks. If your sleep problem persists, don't ignore it! Seek help.[5] Treatments for sleep disruption are plenteous, and restoration of this daily rhythm is perhaps the most important thing you can do to set the tone for good daily rhythms.

## Skill: Notice Your Rhythms

Tim and Candice were fighting during their couples session. Candice complained, "This happens every year! We can't stand each other by

November because I've just ended my training season, which comes right after your ministry's fall push. We have no easy weekends for about ten weeks, and you wind up resenting me for it, forgetting that I pick up the slack during your busy season!"

Tim countered, "Your busy season is longer. And I wind up doing more of the soccer-practice driving because of your workouts."

"Oh, so you're keeping track? What am I supposed to do, quit running?"

Tim deflated a bit. "Of course I don't want you to quit. I hadn't really thought of how you're picking up the slack during our hectic beginning-of-the-school-year student-ministry time. We just have our busy seasons back to back. When I'm tired, I forget that."

You'd be surprised by how many marriage conflicts could be avoided if people were more aware of and intentional about the pre-dictable rhythms in their lives. When Tim and Candice paused to consider what their fall schedules were like, they appreciated each other's partnership during their push times. Our work together involved making sure the weeks before and after their back-to-back busy seasons were slower and helped them feel more ready for and recovered from the time of intensity. They made time for luxurious family meals and games and created space for each of them to recoup in a solitary retreat. People get into trouble when they stumble into rhythms and seasons without noticing what will be required of them. Planning well for intense times and living into times of ease can help your inner world feel better overall.

David is one of my dear clients who needed a better weekly rhythm. He is a true weekend warrior, living for the times he can escape the city and do the hiking and water sports that he loves. His sales job suits him well, but his real passion is being outdoors. In the truest sense, he works to live, rather than the other way around. He noticed that on Mondays and Tuesdays his mood was low and his anxiety high. Wednesdays tended to be a little easier. By Thursday, he felt steady and upbeat as he looked forward to the weekend.

Adding things that brought an influx of happy hormones to David's Mondays and Tuesdays was exceedingly helpful. He and his wife changed their show-watching night to Monday, giving him something to look forward to that involved fun and cuddling, both of which helped his hormone soup. He also altered his morning routine to accommodate a longer run outside on those days. Endorphins from exercising and being in nature made the beginning of the week more enjoyable. These changes to David's weekly rhythm really helped.

How could you benefit from analyzing your weekly, monthly, and yearly rhythms? If you can observe them, you can better prepare for them.

PRACTICE THE SKILL
## *Notice Your Rhythms*

1. *Reflect.* Consider your weekly, monthly, and yearly rhythms within each category listed below (recognizing that you may benefit from reflecting on your annual rhythms separately from thinking about your weekly and monthly rhythms):

   - work projects and deadlines
   - vacations
   - school, sports, and activity seasons
   - holidays
   - hobbies
   - church

- the interplay of your rhythms with those of key people in your life (family members, housemates, close friends, and others)
- lulls or slow times
- mood trends
- anxious times
- bored times

2. *Evaluate.*

- What do you like in what you see?
- What do you dislike?
- How is the mix of rhythms?
- Is there a balance of busy times and slow times?
- Are there "glut" times (when lots of things converge at once)?
- If there are times of low mood, do you also experience better mood seasons?
- What is fixed and what is flexible?
- What do you want more of, and what do you want less of?
- Are you trying to do too much? Or too much at one time?
- Do you notice trends in your moods? (For example, think of David's happy and low times at predictable parts of the week.)

3. *Plan.*

- Given the rhythms that are already in place in your life, how can you plan well for seasons of intensity?

- How can you take advantage of seasons of ease?
- Do you or your family need more support during certain times of the year? What could that look like? (For example, would you benefit from childcare or other services? More support from friends, practically or emotionally? Something else?)

When one of my closest friends considered taking on a large ministry role in our church, she asked if I'd support her as she entered the challenge. I agreed to pray for her and check in with her as she settled into this new leadership role. One of my clients plans a family weekend in the woods for hiking and games before the beginning of the kids' sports season, when they'll rarely be able to have dinner together. These are just two of many ways to plan well for intense seasons.

## Skill: Create New Rhythms

Parenting had never been harder. My daughter, Brenna, was in a phase of unparalleled rage outbursts, almost all of which were directed toward me. In the limited vocabulary of an eleven-year-old, she could only get so far with cursing, but the vitriol was real, and it cut deep. At the same time, we were battling the county, asking them to fund specialized schooling for Brenna. Hours-long meetings left me battered and bereft. The difficult fight with the county seemed to be met with an even more painful fight at home as my daughter's school stress oozed into every corner of our family's life.

"Only two more weeks," I said to my husband while slumped on the couch next to him after a particularly difficult evening.

"You're on the major countdown to Susie time now. You're almost there."

He smiled at me, understanding the powerful anchor my fall

and spring trips with my college roommate had become. As I mentioned in the last chapter, these visits are times for both of us to debrief—in as much detail as we want—the events of the previous six months. We offer support, perspective, and prayer to one another. Over the years, we've become experts in the patterns and movements of God in one another's lives. Those visits are a sustaining and essential rhythm for me, one that I've recommended to dozens of parents (and demanded from a handful of special-needs parents). The time is a distinct break from the rhythm of parenting a special-needs child. The cadence and energy slow and flow differently in my Susie times, which have become an important reset for me over the years. I'm not sure what my hormone soup would have been like without it!

### Closing the Stress Cycle

In the book *Burnout*, Emily Nagoski and Amelia Nagoski talk about the importance of closing the stress cycle. What they mean by this is that our bodies naturally rev up for stressful situations, but we need the cycle of stress to complete so that our bodies go back to their baseline state.[6] Sometimes, people live in such a way that the stress cycle doesn't complete, which causes chronic stress-hormone problems. Creating rhythms like my Susie time is a way to complete the stress cycle even when my day-to-day life is unchanged. Psalm 80:18 says, "Revive us so we can call on your name once more." Closing the stress cycle does this. It revives and restores us so that we can call on God again and refocus our efforts. And in that particularly hard year when Brenna was suffering so intensely and we were pressing for education funding, my three-day reprieve did just that. I came home ready and invigorated, able to reenter my life in a better state.

Doing this is as important as having regular medical check-ups! And honestly, creating these rhythms may *prevent* the need for so many doctors' visits because the benefit of completing the stress cycle on a regular basis helps our bodies' digestion, immune systems, and yes, hormones![7] On a day-to-day basis, the skills of having better breaks, mornings, and bedtimes all help you close the stress cycle in the daily and weekly rhythms of your life. For your larger life rhythms, closing the stress cycle will take some creativity. You'll need to take your personality into account because what's needed to close the stress cycle looks different for different people. An old friend, Gil, is deeply introverted. His challenging job and active family life stretch his relational capacity to the absolute maximum. His essential yearly rhythms include two-week solo backpacking trips and eight-day silent retreats. Another friend, Oma, escapes her quiet family for a raucous week with loud, fun-loving friends at a theme park each year, a vacation that her family would hate!

---

PRACTICE THE SKILL
## Create New Rhythms

1. *Reflect.* What are some draining things in your life that could be balanced with opposing energy? Here are some examples.

   - You're initiating all the time and would love a rhythm of having things planned for you. Or the opposite—your life is routine, and you'd like a rhythm of spontaneity.

- Your work is very heavy, and you'd like a rhythm of levity.
- Your work doesn't take advantage of your intellect, so you'd like a rhythm of learning.
- You're in ministry and leading everything spiritual that you're part of; you need a rhythm of being led spiritually.
- Your life is very solitary, and you'd benefit from a rhythm of community (or vice versa).

Where in your life do you need rhythms that close the stress cycle? Consider these examples, but apply the concept to your unique situation.

- Your family life is taxing, and you need breaks (something like my Susie times, perhaps?).
- You have intense seasons of work, ministry, or volunteering, and a celebration could close the stress cycle.
- Your stress at work is unrelenting. Closing the stress cycle might mean periodically scheduling time off so your brain, body, and soul can recover.
- Other seasons of intensity: helping your child with college applications, recovering from surgery, moving to a new state, taking final exams . . . Do something to mark the end of the season and close the stress cycle.

2. *Evaluate.* Once you've come up with areas of your life that could use opposing energy or closing of the stress cycle, sit in silence around this in God's presence.

- What emotions, desires, and/or ideas are stirring?
- Might adding a new rhythm to your year make sense?

3. *Dream.*

- What could this new rhythm (or these new rhythms) look like?
- Whom can you talk to about this who will be supportive and creative?

4. *Plan.*

- When can this fit into the other rhythms of your weeks, months, or year?
- What financial adjustments need to be made to make this happen?
- Which people need to buy in on this plan?

• • • • •

Mara seemed flat and directionless. Frankly, I was a bit bored with our sessions. After working through some significant relationship issues with her mother, Mara was reluctant to end therapy. But she didn't have a clear view of what to work on. Her job as an office manager was steady and satisfying. She was an empty nester, divorced many years earlier, who led a small group for moms of young children. In a revealing conversation, I asked, "What excites you?"

She looked at me blankly and said, "I'm pretty sure the answer to that question is nothing."

"Nothing?"

"Nothing. I feel like I'm in *Groundhog Day*. Since the situation with my mother calmed down, I'm left with . . ." she looked at the floor, shaking her head, and continued, "a very nice, calm, uneventful life."

"What's it like to consider that?"

"A little sad. Has the most exciting thing in my life over the last year really been fighting with my mother?"

"Has it?"

"I think so." Mara's brow furrowed. "I'm not okay with that!"

"Well then, let's get excited!"

Mara had to work hard to find something that gave her a lift. She'd become accustomed to heaviness, having worked through a messy divorce and its aftermath, launched children into the world, and, more recently, fought with her mother. Work had chugged along, as had ministry involvement and friendships, but now Mara sensed an invitation to find a new kind of energy. She reflected, investigated, and prayed. Bit by bit, clarity came. A few weeks after our initial discussion about excitement, she came to our session with some exciting news.

"I've been accepted!"

"To the Enneagram Cohort?" I asked. I knew she'd been waiting to hear back.

"Yes! When I saw the email, I was shaking. I wasn't sure about even opening it because I knew I'd be crushed if I wasn't accepted. When I saw that I was in, I laughed and wept and shouted."

"Sounds like excitement to me!"

Mara's eyes twinkled. "I can't tell you how good this feels! There are four gatherings over the year, and having them on my calendar makes me smile. I've already started on the readings and assignments for the first session! I haven't done this kind of writing and reflecting in years. Janice, I *really* needed this. Before, when I looked ahead, everything seemed so flat. Now this upcoming year is appealing."

Mara's discovery of how to add rhythm to her life ended our work together. She checks in periodically and reports not only becoming an Enneagram junkie but also finding other interests. She started biking, volunteering, and even dating. Something really unlocks when we develop rhythms that give us better-tasting soup.

Mara needed a lift, while Bella needed more slowness. Both created new, life-changing rhythms. It's easy to coast, getting caught up in whatever life brings. If we don't work at it, we can fall into living life reactively, unconsciously believing ourselves to be victims of whatever is happening. I pray that this book will forever change that for you. If you do the work outlined here, you can become an expert chef of your hormone soup. You can experiment with rhythms that suit the situation. You can become like Jesus, whose flexible rhythms kept him connected to the Father *and* energized for ministry. A highly personalized set of rhythms is the best gift you can give yourself, an act of kindness to your body and soul.

Many forces are at work
stealing fulfillment
from your life.

Jesus wants you to have
a rich and satisfying life.

Our choices are key to whether
we experience fulfillment.

By the end of this chapter,
you will know *why*.

# CHAPTER EIGHT

# Living a Life of Fulfillment

Jorge plops down on the couch, sighing. His playfully flopping hair is damp from a recent shower. He fumbles with his shoulder bag a moment, retrieving a take-out box while juggling a coffee cup in his other hand.

"Sorry I'm late. I hadn't eaten anything, so I picked up some food."

Jorge had texted this to me already, and I wasn't surprised. Sessions with Jorge often felt jammed into his overfull life.

"No worries. You know my policy: Bring food and drink. Be comfortable."

He nods, taking a bite of his burrito bowl, talking out of the corner of his mouth.

"My wife told me to talk to you about how disconnected I am from the kids and her."

I cringe inwardly. A spouse's agenda isn't my favorite starting place for a session. But I'm a bit curious. Jorge's frazzled appearance makes me wonder if the slower, more thoughtful Jorge I occasionally sit with in session shows up much in the rest of his life.

After swallowing another bite, he continues. "If she had her way, this is how my evenings would be: I'd cook dinner or clean up the kitchen afterward. And by 'cleaning up the kitchen,' I mean wiping away crumbs, taking the garbage out, putting the placemats away . . . not just washing the dishes. Oh, and dinner would have included an hour of conversation after we finish eating at minute fourteen. Then we'd play a board game as a family, have bath time for the kids, and then have a luxurious bedtime, where each child would get personal parent time reading their favorite stories. When the kids fell asleep, I'd talk with her for an hour."

Jorge looks a bit startled as he realizes that his volume has increased to near shouting. He looks down at his lunch, a bit embarrassed, and reflects, "I mean, who can do all that? Maybe on vacation, but there's just no way!"

As Jorge continues focusing on his lunch, I gather myself, trying to listen to God. *Where should this conversation go?* I wonder.

"Jorge, what do you really want?"

"I want my wife to understand that what *she* wants is impossible! I have ten thousand things to do every night!"

I pause, checking in again with God, then ask, "What do you really want?"

Frustrated, he rests his lunch on the side table and wipes his mouth, and I can see him shifting into a slower space. He closes his eyes for a moment, then responds, "I don't know what you mean."

Gently, I repeat, "What do you really want?"

He gets it. We aren't going to troubleshoot his evening routine or psychoanalyze his wife's unreasonableness. Not right now. Jorge's mouth twitches as he wrestles with the tears that threaten to come.

"I want . . . I want to feel better than this. I want to feel like I'm living the life I'm supposed to be living. What my wife said . . . I want to be connected, but I don't know how. At the end of the day, I just want to get stuff done and shut down."

He looks up at me, eyes bright with tears, and continues, "I have everything I've ever wanted: wonderful wife, beautiful kids, my dream job, and money enough to get to the beach each year. But I keep feeling like I need a break from all of them. Like they're getting in the way or something. I can't believe I'm saying this. I have all I want, but I don't know how to *connect* with it all. I feel like I'm constantly just trying to keep everything going."

"What do you really want?" I ask.

"I want life to feel like it's supposed to feel," Jorge responds. "I'm just so empty. How can that be, when my life is filled to the brim?"

## The Fulfilled Life

In John 10:9-10, Jesus says, "Yes, I am the gate. Those who come in through me will be saved. They will come and go freely and will find good pastures. The thief's purpose is to steal and kill and destroy. *My purpose is to give them a rich and satisfying life*" (emphasis added). Another translation says, "I have come that they may have life, and have it to the full" (NIV). I dearly love this passage. It encourages me to consider what a rich, satisfying, and full life would mean and to cling to the understanding that Jesus wants that for me. Now. While I'm alive. To summarize, Jesus wants us to experience the gift of a fulfilling life, and that gift is being stolen, killed, and destroyed. The thief in this passage is quite literally a sheep robber, or later in the passage, a wolf. Metaphorically, however, the "thief" may be the enemy of Jesus, whether that is Satan or other forces of darkness set on destruction. Many of my clients feel the impact of a less-than-fulfilling life but don't understand the forces at work making fulfillment difficult so don't know what to do about it.

> Jesus wants us to experience the gift of a fulfilling life, and that gift is being stolen, killed, and destroyed.

The battle for a fulfilling life is won in the moment-to-moment choices that add up to rich and satisfying hours, which add up to rich and satisfying days, which add up to rich and satisfying weeks, which add up to . . . get my point?

We can have a job that suits us perfectly but fail to make the choices that make our dream job fulfilling.

We may marry the love of our life but fail to make the choices that bring the connection and intimacy that make the relationship fulfilling.

A rich, satisfying, and fulfilling life is well worth having but isn't necessarily easy to attain in our day-to-day and hour-to-hour living. Often, we don't know *how* to choose fulfillment over momentary pleasure or distraction. We may have dozens of chances to select fulfillment but miss most of them. I see clients who know endless amounts about passing time but who don't know the first thing about pursuing fulfillment—*in a given day*. This is true for many of us. In other words, the way we live day to day is the enemy who is stealing, killing, and destroying true fulfillment.

I'm not immune to this. If a client cancels and I have an unexpected free hour, I *know* that taking a walk and giving my body and brain a break would be fulfilling, but I often choose to scroll through my phone instead. It's easier and feels more pleasant in the moment to slide into the numbness that only my phone can bring. But at the end of the hour, I'll either feel truly refreshed by a walk or I'll feel dulled by my newsfeed and social media. Or, as I reflect on today, I was half an hour late starting my writing time because I was sucked into clickbait. I read an entire article about the death of the world's tallest dog. Why? I got lured in by my kryptonite: a doggie picture. But all that article has done for me is taken time away from what I've committed to do! It was pleasurable in the moment, but *not fulfilling.* Ultimately, that choice went against self-care because it put off my whole schedule by thirty minutes and robbed me of doing as much writing as I needed to do to keep my deadline. If I had written first and then discerned whether I had time for the dog article afterward, I would have felt much better—more fulfilled.

It isn't always the phone that pulls at me. I've been avoiding doing a deep dive on a couple with whom I've been working for a while. A "deep dive" is what I call thoroughly examining a couple who is stuck in treatment. I seem to be having the same conversation with this couple over and over. I feel frustrated, they seem hopeless . . . I need to look more closely: reread my notes, look for themes, remember forgotten history, see which skills we have—and haven't—covered. I need to sit in quiet and listen for my instincts, ask for the Spirit's guidance, and deeply consider a path forward. This is hard work! And I'm avoiding it, plain and simple. When I have time, I do every other possible chore on my list. I'd rather do easy things. But I'm bothered by not doing this work, and I *know* I'd feel competent and proud of myself if I'd do it. Especially when my next session with the couple rolls around. In other words, it'd be fulfilling *if I'd only stop avoiding it!*

Few of us consider how day-to-day choices like these might affect our overall fulfillment. More often, people look only at the big picture.

In another session with Jorge, we are hard at work exploring the empty feelings he is experiencing. This day Jorge is frustrated with work. I start the session as I typically do: "Jorge, what is your inner world like today?"

"Not great. Frazzled, busy, tired . . . I thought that getting my dream job would clear all this up. Work is just like home. It ought to feel better because this is more aligned with what I enjoy. Only . . . I'm not enjoying it."

"Tell me more."

Jorge continues, describing how he feels empty, sick of his growing to-do list, and impatient with colleagues, as well as how he thinks that expectations are unreasonable. He just got this job four months ago and was thrilled to find it! He is working with a nonprofit creating internship programs at local businesses for at-risk youth. He continually talks about how satisfying the job is, but he also flounders with the lack of structure in his days.

"Maybe I should go back to school and go in a new direction. Maybe I'm just not in the right career."

"Wait up, Jorge. Can we stay on what you were saying before? You just went through a career change that got you to this job through a solid discernment process. I was with you when you were deciding this. I remember how thoughtful, prayerful, and grounded you were. You with me?"

"I suppose so, but it just seems like it should feel different from this."

"I hear you. And maybe you are off track. But before we jump on that train, could we start by examining a typical day and week at work and home, then go from there?"

We go through his calendar to piece together a typical day for Jorge. We see a few themes:

- a stressful work life (feeling chronically behind and not knowing how to start or finish his tasks there)
- a frenzied personal life (chasing after his three children, scant meaningful interactions with his wife, little substantial contact with friends)
- going to bed without accomplishing what he hoped to that day, either at home or at work

Jorge is befuddled. He loves his family and is financially stable. He has his dream job after changing from a steady-but-misaligned education job with the state. Now he feels that what he does at work every day is more aligned with who he wants to be. So why doesn't he feel better?

I suspect that he doesn't know how to fix the small problems in his day, which will lead to more fulfillment overall. He is such a visionary person that he tends to focus on the big pieces of his life without addressing the smaller aspects of how he is living day to day.

"Jorge, do you remember that session when we talked through how to arrange your workday?"

"Yes," he says. "And do you remember how I didn't do it?"

"Um . . . yes. That's just an example. It seems like we've had many similar conversations. I'm curious how you'd feel if you'd make some of those changes. I think your empty feeling may be tied to your understanding of daily self-care."

He slowly starts to nod.

"Let's talk."

| EMPTY DAY | FULFILLING DAY |
|---|---|
| reactive | proactive |
| disjointed | purposeful |
| disappointed | satisfied |
| disconnected | connected |

Jorge is not alone. After four or five empty-feeling days, any of us would be down, even if all the big pieces of our life were in place. No one's inner world feels wonderful if that's the case. We tend to lose chances at fulfillment in the small choices we make, and *they build up*, wearing us down and causing us to become confused about whether the life we've chosen is the life we want.

Here are some more examples of how I've seen clients lose chances at fulfillment lately:

- I have a new couple whose connection with each other is anemic and faltering. When I suggested a checking-in exercise that would take about ten minutes per day, both insisted that they don't know where they'd incorporate it into their jam-packed days of work and parenting. But they admit that they watch a couple of hours of Netflix in the evening after the kids go to bed. What might be fulfilling in the long term—growing their connection with each other—is in direct competition with what is preferable in the moment—watching TV.

- A newly minted professor bemoans how little he reads the relevant journal articles that would help him keep sharp in his field even though he truly loves reading. A few minutes later, he tells me how proud he is that he just surpassed his goal of one thousand games of chess in a year, up from eight hundred the previous year. I'm unclear how fulfilling chess is for my client, but I know that he doesn't play the speed version. The hours are very real.

- A Christian leader sighs and explains her intense longing for better rhythms of prayer and contemplation. She even weeps a bit as she tells me how much more grounded and alive she feels when she's more connected to God. I wonder whether to bring up last week's conversation about her daily Pinterest activity, which she confessed is obsessive. Will she see how her time could be shifted from an activity that leaves her feeling empty to one that would fulfill her? Will she be open to me raising this?

Each of these dear clients is trading in fulfillment for momentary pleasure, and Jorge fits into this mold. Reimagining self-care would allow all of them to see the wonderful invitation. Jesus tells us, "My yoke is easy to bear, and the burden I give you is light" (Matthew 11:30). It isn't oppressive to choose the difficult option if it gives you more internal stability and joy. Keeping momentary pleasures (whether checking our newsfeeds, playing another round of chess, or watching another hour of Netflix) within certain boundaries for the sake of fulfillment is gratifying when we see our growing ability to accomplish things that are important to us. It's hard to do this without intentional effort when a universe of distraction is at our fingertips at all times, not to mention our desire to avoid things we don't want to do (even if we know they're good for us, like my "deep dive" for the client couple). But we need to understand the problem so we can see what makes life so difficult to manage.

Let's examine two underlying tensions to enhance our ability to practice better self-care: (1) focus versus distraction and (2) short-term preferences versus fulfillment.

## Focus versus Distraction

As Jorge and I start examining how his days tend to unfold, we discuss how he plans the many meetings he leads in a typical week.

"How long does it take you to prep for a two-hour staff meeting like the one you're describing?"

"I don't know. It seems like I'm never finished prepping for stuff like that. I get so distracted."

This sounds all too familiar, in my own life and with many clients I've worked with recently. I know what to ask next. "Where is your phone while you are prepping?"

"Right next to me."

"And about how many times do you think you're drawn to it while you're working?"

"I suppose as many times as I see a text or notification come in. Ten? Twenty? But it's more than that. I also pick it up when I feel stuck in my prep."

"So how much time would you say you spend on your phone during an hour you're trying to plan the meeting?"

Jorge lets his head fall back on my couch, then exhales sharply and closes his eyes.

"At least half the time. Maybe more. Oh no, I'm like a teenager! What's wrong with me?"

"Jorge, hang in there. No one is immune to the pull of the phone. Let's keep looking at this. What's going on when you pick up the phone?"

"Well, notices grab my attention, but . . . also when I'm feeling a little anxious or lost in my planning, I grab the phone habitually. It distracts me from that tension."

"And what if you didn't grab your phone?"

160

"I'd probably just push through and finish a lot faster. When I pick up my phone, sometimes it leads me on a fifteen-minute click-fest! I read articles and respond to tweets and get completely off topic."

"About how long might it take you to plan a meeting without your phone available?"

"Probably thirty minutes, depending on what I'm trying to do with the team. Oh man, this is embarrassing."

"Hey, hey . . . please know that I'm not trying to shame you. I have to do these inventories on myself, and there's hardly anyone out there who wouldn't be challenged by this."

My trainings with groups confirm this. The pull of distraction from sustained focus has become a challenge for nearly every person that I've worked with in the past few years. For some, working in a focused way isn't a lost art—it's never been developed! No wonder preparing meetings has become overwhelming. With distractions built in, Jorge and folks like him assume that planning a meeting might take several hours because, well, it does. With a dozen or more phone pickups during an hour of work, a task that would take one hour with focused attention stretches into two, three, or more. What could be fulfilling—having the meeting prepared—turns into an on-going, anxiety-producing spin that can last for days, until the meeting happens. All for the sake of phone checks. In my estimation, it isn't worth it. Reimagined self-care looks different. It means developing our capacity for sustained focus because our souls are more fulfilled when we accomplish the tasks at hand.

It isn't just our phones that distract us. Remember the earlier chapters in this book on thoughts? Intrusive thoughts can lead us to cognitive bunny trails that pull us out of focused work. And then there are interruptions of all sorts that can work against us having sustained focus. Distractions rob us of a rich and satisfying moment, hour, or afternoon. I emphasize phones because for most of us (though not all), changing phone habits will create the biggest shift in a sense of hour-to-hour, day-to-day fulfillment. I have no intention of giving up my phone, and I don't expect that you will either. But *the way we deal with our phones represents* the *most practical and real challenge to moment-to-moment and hour-to-hour fulfillment.* Depending on how we interact with our phones, those small metal boxes in our pockets may be what steals, kills, and destroys our focus on the things we're called to do. Or they can be what they're intended to be, convenient tools in this modern age.

## Short-Term Preferences versus Fulfillment

When the pandemic started, our daughter, Brenna, came home from her independence-development program for young adults with special needs. As we suffered from the loss of many pleasurable activities during lockdown, I was desperate for my family to cooperate with my attempts to cope. One evening I was feeling particularly antsy. I wanted to do something interactive . . . with humans . . . in the flesh, not on screen. I wanted to play a game, and my daughter was not having it. While she lived away from home, her daily rhythm had been established: In the evenings, she watched videos and chatted online. A board game was *not* a welcome deviation from that preferred activity, no matter how desperate I felt for human interaction. Our conversation went something like this:

> *Brenna*: "I don't feel like playing."
> *Me*: "Please? It'll be fun once you get into it!"

*Brenna*: "Go play with Owen [her brother]. I want to watch this video."

*Me*: "I've got Owen and Dad on board, but the game requires four players. You're all we've got!"

*Brenna*: "Well, go do something else. I want to have fun."

*Me*: "But I've done everything else there is to do, and I'm going crazy. I just want to laugh with you all and be playful. *Please!!!*"

*Brenna*: "But the good stuff uploads at night, and I don't want to wait to watch it."

*Me*: "Would you take a bribe?"

*Brenna*: "How much?"

Sound familiar, anyone? Eventually, I did negotiate for game nights with Brenna. She wound up having a great time because we were doing something together—teasing, laughing, and competing—which made us feel connected and fulfilled. Playing games together was satisfying in a way that watching videos alone couldn't be. Too often, we trade in fulfillment for momentary pleasure. Reimagined self-care means upending this gravitational pull, which affects all of us.

Sadly, the pursuit of short-term preferences follows us into every corner of our lives, even parenting. We unwittingly teach our children to avoid potentially fulfilling experiences because we can't stand to see them suffer through hard challenges. This came up in a recent conversation with a woman named Kate, where she shared a dilemma she and her husband were facing.

They'd become reluctant to allow their children to spend unsupervised time with her parents because the kids were often frustrated at their grandparents' house; they got bored and didn't like their grandpa's cooking. The grandparents expected that, for the most part, children should entertain themselves and eat the food they're served. They weren't very open to Kate's suggestions of new recipes or outings that her children would enjoy. Instead, they continued to have the kids play on their own or join them in playing rummy or doing a jigsaw puzzle. They also brought the kids along on their evening dog walks. Kate's kids found these activities boring, and Kate was sick of their complaints. As we discussed this dilemma, I could tell I was pushing some buttons.

"Kate, it may not be bad for your kids to have to navigate these difficulties with their grandparents."

"But they don't like playing cards or eating meat loaf! My parents are so clueless."

"That is likely quite true. But what bothers you about your kids suffering a bit in their grandparents' care?"

"Well . . ." she paused. "It's the whining! I can't stand the complaining, and I just want it to stop. It should be fun to be with their grandparents, and I hate that the kids are so miserable. They have a great time with my husband's parents! They order pizza, watch movies, and go out for ice cream."

"Let's take this another step. If you could endure the whining, would there be any benefits to your kids learning to be with your parents?"

"Aren't kids supposed to love being with their grandparents? They shouldn't be made to suffer through it, right?"

At this point in the conversation, I felt myself floundering a bit. I wanted her kids to have fun with their grandparents too! But I steadied myself, realizing that Kate was caught in a mindset that wasn't serving her or her children.

"And what if they suffer through it?"

"They won't look forward to being with their grandparents."

"You're right, they might need some coaching on how to handle that . . . Could that be okay?"

"I don't know. I feel like I should keep them home and spare us the complaining. And aren't I supposed to protect them from feeling bad?"

"Well, if you believe it's your job to make sure your kids don't feel bad, then perhaps yes. But may I challenge that?"

Kate looked at me, debating. I could see what was happening. She wasn't just reluctant to have her kids suffer through something unpleasant—she also didn't want to endure their complaining. Finally, she decided. "Yes, I want you to challenge that."

"Bear with me. I'd suggest that it's *good* for your kids to navigate visits with their grandparents. It's good for them to grow in their ability to do things they don't prefer, especially for the sake of important things like relationships. If they can learn to do this, it will prepare them for real life. It's good for them to know that there are fun grandparents and there are less-fun grandparents, and that there's value in being in relationship with both kinds! If they learn this as kids, then they'll be more prepared for the future: dealing with a difficult roommate, or supporting a friend who is going through something hard, or eating plain food for the sake of honoring a host who lacks the means for an elaborate meal."

I wondered how this was landing with Kate; she was looking at me intensely. Then she offered, "I literally *never* think like that. I'm always just trying to make everyone happy in the moment, including myself."

"I hear you. It's hard to think any other way."

I remember what a revolution it was to be challenged similarly when my kids were young. In the remarkable book *Gist: The Essence of Raising Life-Ready Kids*, psychologist Michael W. Anderson and pediatrician Timothy D. Johanson explain that

> kids need to have a certain number of these not-so-positive experiences in order to mature and gain wisdom and perspective. Without these kinds of experiences children may grow up unprepared for adult life. We see this all the time in our respective practices—young adults whose maturity levels are sluggishly behind their chronological ages, and who have little ability to function as emancipated adults.[1]

Maturing requires learning to forsake your preference for the sake of fulfilling things like community and friendship. This value is only developed when people engage in less-preferred activities and see that there's a fulfilling payoff. If Kate's kids never have to make this choice when they're young, how will they have this life-essential skill as adults? Kate has some reckoning to do. Is she willing to choose the harder path in order to develop her kids' capacity to live richer, more satisfying lives? Is she willing to show them how to lean in, even in situations that don't reflect their preferences?

A fulfilling life goes against bold attempts by advertisers, marketers, and who-knows-who-else to convince us that we should have everything we want when we want it. Instant gratification has become our assumed right! Over time the impact of this is devastating. Our days are full of things that give us instant gratification . . . and we're left wondering why we feel so empty. A fulfilling life means keeping our values and goals constantly top of mind, informing our moment-to-moment choices.

• • ● • •

My neighborhood book club had a meeting recently. I felt very behind on writing and a myriad of other tasks at the time, and I was sorely tempted to skip. I had the perfect excuse: I hadn't read the book. But I was working on this chapter, which caused me to pause. I'm committed to building long-term friendships with the women in my book club. The short-term relief I might have felt in plowing through some tasks probably wouldn't have been as fulfilling as valuing the friendships. So I chose to attend. And it was very, very nice. At the end of the evening, my soul felt restored. The following day, during a canceled session that felt like a divine intervention, I buckled down. So I ended up getting some of the tasks checked off my list too.

Moment by moment.

Hour by hour.

That's how fulfillment works. The rich and satisfying life that Jesus wants for us doesn't happen magically. It takes intention and effort, every day.

A fulfilling life is the
best self-care imaginable.

Fulfillment requires
intentional effort.

Jesus wants you to
live a life of fulfillment.

By the end of this chapter,
you will know *how*.

# CHAPTER NINE

# Fulfillment:
# The Essential Skills

The fuzzy Christmas throw I'd purchased sat on a table near the front door. I'd bought it for my friend Katie, who'd adored the blanket at my house the previous year. I'd felt so clever about finding one for her, but now the blanket accused me—how could I have let so many days go by without taking it to her? We were well into Advent. I remembered the pile of ornaments I'd never delivered the previous year, which robbed me of Christmas cheer. As the blanket caught my eye, I sighed and considered my schedule, just as I'd done the last several days, not sure when the twenty-minute trip to her house could fit. The irony of writing about making life more fulfilling while struggling to deliver a gift I was excited about wasn't lost on me, and I determined that this would be the day I'd make it a priority. I grabbed the blanket, made the drive, and knocked on the door. It was so gratifying to see Katie's face light up with delight. Later that day she texted me a picture of herself and her young son cuddling under the blanket. I felt such joy!

It can be hard to squeeze small yet fulfilling things into our busy lives. Without some determination, that blanket might have stayed on the table until Lent! Often we skip fulfilling experiences because we aren't intentional enough. Our task now is to figure out how to live more fulfilled lives hour to hour and day to day. Remember, you can have all the big pieces in place but still need major work in some of these areas. Essential skills for living a more fulfilling life include taking time away from your phone, working more effectively, becoming better at pleasure and celebrating, and creating your own "fulfillment ingredients" list. Let's get started!

## Skill: Stop Acting like an Obsessive Lover of Your Phone

By challenging readers to consider how their phones may interfere with a fulfilling life, I run the risk of people immediately writing me off. Please allow me to clarify.

I am not a phone hater.

I'm grateful for the convenience mine brings me.

I'm more connected to more of the important people in my life because of my phone.

It brings me incalculable joy that my photos are accessible at all times.

I love my Bitmoji; she expresses me so well.

My son, Owen, and I play Word Hunt. We keep a running score, which is fun.

I love my phone. But I don't want to relate to it like an obsessive lover. Do these behaviors sound familiar?

- checking in with it many times an hour just because
- neurotically needing it to be near you at all times

- feeling irritated and uncomfortable without it in your hand, pocket, or nearby bag
- being unable or unwilling to go any period of time without access to it
- experiencing lostness and longing in situations where you don't have phone access
- wondering what's going on and feeling a compulsion to pick your phone up

When we frame it this way, it *is* a bit scary how attached we can become to our phones! I did some research and found that

- "on average, Americans check their phones 344 times per day," and
- "Americans spend an average of **2 hours and 54 minutes on their phones each day**,"
- which totals forty-four days spent on our phones in a year.[1]
- And 31 percent of Americans report going online "almost constantly."[2]

I'm a contributor to these statistics. When I'm not extremely intentional about disciplining myself, I easily log sixty-five phone pickups per day (there's this horrifying place on iPhones where you can see your daily pickups). I get glued to my phone as if I'm some sort of jealous lunatic! *What's in there? What am I missing? Help me! Be with me. Tell me I'm special. Ask me to the prom . . .* Well, maybe not the last one, but this does remind me of a few high school obsessions.

Just like Jorge, each time I pick up my phone I'm letting my attention shift from whatever I'm doing to whatever I see there. Whatever boundaries I give myself are effective for a time, but then my pickup rate slowly trends upward again. I find myself needing to start over again and again to maintain limits.

Many medical experts are reluctant to use the word *addiction* in relation to anything other than substance misuse, but mental health professionals talk about compulsive phone behaviors because many of our clients struggle with this. And smartphone overuse has similarities to behavioral addictions like compulsive gambling.[3] This means that when we pick up our phones at any given time, we can't predict what they will bring us. Will it be a jarring or scary headline? If so, we'll receive a jolt of stress hormones. Will it be a text from a friend or a notification that our post has seventy-five likes? If so, we'll receive a jolt of happy hormone. Because we don't know what we'll see each time, phone pickups are variably reinforcing. In addiction-treatment circles, we know that smartphone overuse is a tricky addiction to treat, much like gambling. (With alcohol and most drugs, the reinforcement is at least predictable.)

Most of us can relate to habitually grabbing our phones in quiet moments, when feeling stumped while working, or when feeling lonely, anxious, or uncomfortable. After all, who wants to be the only person in a waiting room with nothing in their hands? How strange we'd seem to everyone glued to their phones. Except they wouldn't even notice.

The reason I address this so thoroughly in this chapter is that these constant interruptions and shifts of focus can disrupt our sense of fulfillment. We don't work as efficiently, so we get less done. We get distracted from our friends and family in conversation, so we feel less connected. We have fewer spaces of true solitude, so we feel less comfortable with ourselves. All these things—and many more phone-related behaviors—can decrease our capacity to experience rich and satisfying lives.

So how do we stop our obsessive phone behaviors?

## *Phone Pickup Challenge*

I invite you to participate in what I call the "phone pickup challenge." (I just stopped myself from reaching for my phone *right now* as I felt a twinge of uncertainty about what to write next! Whew, this is hard.) It goes like this:

1. *Prepare.* Follow these steps:

    - Check your current phone pickup number. (Google instructions to find "Screen Time" [for iPhone users] or "Digital Wellbeing" [for Android users]. You can also download an app that will count the number of pickups for you.)
    - Identify your most challenging situations. When is the temptation to pick up your phone strongest, and where are you when it occurs?
    - Choose a "phone nest"—a location (perhaps a charging station) you commit to placing your phone sometimes to keep it out of sight.

2. *Create a goal.* Challenge yourself to pick up your phone fewer times. Making a concrete goal helps (when I do this experiment, I normally try to reduce pickups by 50 percent).

3. *Reflect.* Consider these questions:

    - Have you been able to reduce your pickups? If so, what do you notice as you refrain?
    - What subtle emotions move you to grab your phone?

(Try practicing "Feel Your Feels" from the "Emotions: The Essential Skills" chapter.) What is it like to deal with those emotions without your phone?

- Do you notice any difference in your ability to do sustained work?
- Is there another situation or place where you'd like to challenge yourself?

4. *Celebrate.* When you successfully keep your new goal for a whole week, celebrate the accomplishment. You are increasing your chances for fulfillment, one missed pickup at a time!

Doing this challenge makes me more aware of how often I unconsciously reach for the phone when I feel a twinge of discomfort. (This literally just happened. I moved my phone so I won't do this again.) It also makes me realize how lazy I can be about dealing with myself! I feel like the ultimate hypocrite, avoiding the slightest experience of a negative emotion after writing a chapter about how to experience emotions. I work on this kind of stuff nearly every day with clients, and still, this is so hard for me. Engaging in the pickup challenge helps me practice what I preach. When I deal with my emotions directly, I feel steadier and more grounded in Jesus as I practice a breath prayer or offer my current difficulty to him and then carry on with my work.

These phone pickup challenges also help me be more efficient. Ticking things off my to-do list gives me a wonderful sense of efficacy, but being able to rest better in the evening is even more gratifying. Knowing that I've worked well helps me stop dealing with my to-do list, even if I haven't finished everything on it. All this leads to a more fulfilling day.

## Skill: Learn to Work More Effectively

For many years of my career, I've worked with recent college graduates as they've transitioned into becoming campus ministers. We consider an awful lot of adulting at our trainings; how to work is just one. But my, my, my, is it essential. The grads prepare and lead meetings, write talks, plan trainings, and create presentations. It's the kind of work that takes all the time you give it yet rarely allows you to feel finished. Doing all this preparation brings up anxiety, doubt, confusion, and distress. This reality makes knowing how to work well critical. I've worked with other professionals who had been placed on performance-improvement plans because they couldn't complete paperwork or reports on time. Others had been censured for poor presentations that they hadn't adequately prepared for. In most cases, my clients could have done better if they'd focused better during the time they'd had to do the work. It turns out that we aren't like Jesus, who seemed to speak and teach just fine with no preparation that we know of. The rest of us would do well to honor ourselves—and those we're leading—by learning to work more effectively.

PRACTICE THE SKILL
*Focused Work*

Your attention span can be developed with practice, just as it can be diminished by allowing yourself to be continually interrupted.

One *New York Times* reporter noted with horror that his capacity to read long articles was declining. He set out to regain his attention span by practicing focused reading.[4] We can use a similar strategy. Choose a job-related task you need to work on, and follow these five steps.[5]

1. *Set a timer.* Start with manageable chunks of time that aren't too intimidating (try fifteen, thirty, or forty-five minutes).

2. *Move your phone out of reach.* If you're using your phone's timer, make sure you can hear it when it goes off, but keep the phone well out of sight and reach. Notifications may be too tempting to ignore.

3. *Turn off all notifications on your computer.* Close your browser unless you're doing legitimate research as part of your work. If you are, close all other windows.

4. *Resolve to stay on task until the timer goes off,* **no matter how you feel.** (We can easily slide back into our distraction habit if we allow ourselves out of our timed commitment because we feel frustrated, anxious, or discouraged.)

5. *When your timer goes off, take a five- to fifteen-minute break.* Then repeat.

These steps sound obvious, but focused work has become so unusual that nearly everyone is challenged by employing this method. Right now, I'm using this method to write uninterrupted for sixty minutes. Without it, I'd habitually reach for my phone, and my attention would get pulled away from my writing.

## Skill: Do Pleasure Better

Yesterday I was gearing up to go running. Really it was jogging . . . well, let's be honest, plodding (which is a tick up from walking). I digress. I was gearing up to go plodding: leashing the dogs, hunting for my gloves and hat, and considering what to listen to. Part of me was getting ready to listen to my favorite work podcast so I could multitask. While I was scrolling through the episode list, another part of me spoke up. *Janice, you've never been busier than you are right now. Working, writing, and all your other commitments have you going all the time. You'll be "on" for the entire day. Why should you fill your plodding time with information?* This got my attention. I toggled over to Pandora and typed in "You Dropped a Bomb on Me." (Unfamiliar? Take a listen.) Outside I went with funky tunes playing in my ears. Each new song made me smile as I paced myself to "Boogie Shoes" and "Let's Groove."[6] And you know what happened? I deeply enjoyed myself. Also, my plodding might have resembled running as the music motivated me. I moved myself out of a mindset of obligation and into one of true pleasure—and benefitted profoundly.

Don't get me wrong—I love me some podcasts. When I listen at the right time, I experience true pleasure and replenishment. But we all need to understand how to insert true pleasure into each day, and a nerdy podcast was the last thing I needed on a day filled with brainwork. Each of us should endeavor to have some true pleasure every day. This is the kind of self-care that restores our souls.

> Each of us should endeavor to have some true pleasure every day. This is the kind of self-care that restores our souls.

*Better, More Frequent Experiences of Pleasure*

A fulfilling life is a sustainable life. As we learn how to do pleasure better and more often, we prevent ourselves from falling into patterns of half-baked attempts at pleasure followed by falling exhausted into a heap. This is what we so often see with self-care efforts as we tend to understand them today. Someone will see that they're exhausted and frayed, so they plan a massage or a spa day. These are good and pleasurable activities, but if we don't learn how to experience true pleasure day to day, these stopgap attempts to rescue ourselves from overwhelm will come up short.

A fulfilling life is a sustainable life.

Overall fulfillment means knowing how to build truly pleasurable experiences into nearly every day. This will involve upgrading our poor attempts at pleasure that are really avoidance or distraction techniques. How we do this will vary based on what is truly pleasurable to each of us. For instance, some games on my phone are actually very fun for me, while others are just time killers. Reading a novel is pure joy. So is a good workout. For others, those things are torture! They may find pleasure in a warm cup of coffee or listening to a satirist.

PRACTICE THE SKILL
## A Pleasure Examen

Since what constitutes a pleasurable experience varies greatly from person to person, I recommend practicing a "pleasure Examen" for at least one week to discover the things that give you true pleasure and start incorporating them into your daily life.

At the end of each day, consider the following questions and record your answers in your journal, a notebook, or your phone.

- When did you experience true pleasure today?
- What were the circumstances? Was it planned, or did it just happen?
- How did you feel in response to the activity (playful, relaxed, whimsical, satisfied, full, etc.)?
- Was there pleasure that would have been enhanced by better timing or focus?
- Did your pleasurable experience feel balanced with your other commitments?
- If you didn't experience pleasure today, what could you have done differently to enjoy even a small amount?
- What did you learn today about what is truly pleasurable to you?

After seven days, review and evaluate.

- What intentional and unintentional things brought you pleasure in your week?
- What did you learn about yourself from doing the pleasure Examen?
- How much did your pleasure seem to fit with your other commitments?
- How can you maintain a good balance of focused pleasure in your day-to-day life?

Here's what I learned or reaffirmed when I practiced the pleasure Examen:

- Sitting by a fire is just scrumptious for me.
- I always resist doing it, but walking the dog around the block between sessions or before I head home wakes up my senses and leaves me feeling refreshed (yes, my dog comes to work with me).
- I love reading during the day, not only when I'm trying to fall asleep.
- I enjoy the feeling in my muscles after a strength workout.
- Doing nice things for friends and neighbors makes me happy and helps me feel connected.

## Skill: Celebrate More, Celebrate Better

I smiled and took my seat. It was our regional staff conference, an annual event for the group of campus ministers I'd helped train. We were celebrating five- and ten-year milestones of those who were faithfully serving on their various campuses, with speeches and decadent food to mark the occasion. I look forward to these celebrations as a highlight of the year. The longer the individuals have served, the more creative, meaningful, and sometimes silly the speeches are. Everyone knows that their time will come to be celebrated—and to craft a speech for someone else's milestone. When I hear the creativity and thoughtfulness that goes into these speeches, I wonder who is more impacted, the one celebrated or the one celebrating.

I wonder how this ministry team would feel without these celebrations. Less fulfilled, I believe. These annual evenings bond the group and make meaning of the hardship that ministry can bring. It fills us with the inspiration and motivation to get us through the next set of challenges. These carefully crafted celebrations add to the fulfillment of each campus minister as they press on, sharing God's love with college students.

I wonder if that's why God emphasized celebration in the life of Israel so much. They needed to have efforts acknowledged and milestones appreciated so they could keep going when things got hard. Celebrations helped Israel remember times God had worked miracles for them, like the Exodus and the entry into the Promised Land. If you study celebrations in the Old Testament, you'll see that Israel was commanded to party often!

PRACTICE THE SKILL
## Celebrate More and Better

For some of us, celebration is a forgotten art, one that can make a big difference in our sense of fulfillment. I challenge you to begin celebrating more and better! Some people are naturally gifted at celebrating well, while others find it more challenging, depending on personality and temperament. Even if you consider yourself a bad party planner, try stretching yourself a bit in this area. Celebrating can take many different forms, and with some intention, a little can go a long way. Not sure where to start? Here are some helpful steps. I encourage you to write down your answers.

1. *Assess your life for celebrations.*

- When is the last time you really celebrated (yourself, a friend, or a loved one)? Write it down.
- How often do you participate in really good

celebrations? Are you celebrating enough? (For most of us, the answer is no.)

- Look at your life and the people in your immediate circle. What's going on that merits celebration? What are you willing to challenge yourself to do?
- Plan time for celebrations. Get out a calendar and do the hard work.
- Commit to the energy to make these celebrations wonderful. Schedule the time you'll need to make it happen.

2. *Think outside the box.* Ideas for celebrations are endless! Here are just a few:

- Celebrate a child's effort and commitment on their sports team, even if they had a losing season.
- Celebrate the end of finals, the end of a school year, or the completion of a degree.
- If you lead or are on a team at work, celebrate the end of your busy season or the completion of a project.
- After completing anything requiring effort that led to results you can see, celebrate it!

3. *Make your celebrations more fulfilling.*

- *Be clear on what you're celebrating.* Be specific. "We've been married for ten years!" is a bit vague. Really looking at what each person appreciates about the other's efforts in a marriage or acknowledging the changes in the relationship over the years is more specific.

- *Give time and creative energy to planning the celebration.* Even if it's something that happens every year (like a birthday or an anniversary), be thoughtful about what to do during the celebration. Plan in advance (rather than waiting until the last minute) to make it more meaningful.
- *Think creatively.* To celebrate my husband's birthday recently, we had a haiku-writing contest, where friends gave their birthday wishes in humorous verse. That may not be your style, but there are plenty of creative ideas on the internet!
- *Often, celebrating well means creating space to remember.* Each year when I was in campus ministry, we had a senior celebration where each person shared a memory of a time when God had met them. Focused questions that help people reflect are key.

## Skill: Create a Daily Fulfillment Recipe

Gathering data on the state of Jesus' inner world often requires extrapolating, but I believe Jesus probably felt fulfilled at the end of most days. According to the Gospels, his days varied quite a bit. He had busy ministry days, travel days, days with rest, and days with long meals.

Jesus was intentional and flexible. He didn't seem to waste much time or get distracted from his mission. What we do see is that Jesus' life lined up with what was important to him, in the big and small ways.

One way to increase our ability to pursue daily fulfillment is by thinking intentionally about the elements of our days that lead to us feeling fulfilled. For example, I've learned that I want the following ingredients in at least half of my days to feel fulfilled:

- connection with God
- connection with my spouse and kids
- connection with a friend (not necessarily face to face)
- exercise
- focused work (unless I'm on vacation)
- laughter/playfulness/fun that is shared with someone
- time alone
- the experience of pleasure
- the completion of tasks
- the feeling that my work aligns with my call/sense of purpose
- the feeling that I'm not behind on something important
- doing acts of kindness for people
- the feeling that I'm making progress on projects I'm working on
- creating something

I've learned that if I miss any of these ingredients for too long, I begin to feel off-kilter. If I miss many of them over time, I feel empty, lost, and lonely. It isn't pretty.

We've already explored ways we forfeit fulfillment (see pages 162–167 in the previous chapter). I've also found it helpful to identify warning signs that I'm moving away from fulfillment day to day. Here is my list:

- *Feeling regret.* Whether I'm wishing I'd spent my time differently, interacted differently, or chosen to work out, regret helps me know I'm off track.

- *Feeling guilt.* When I find that I haven't reached out to a friend who's hurting, miss an opportunity to connect with a family member, or spend an hour I'd planned to write on Facebook, I know I'm moving away from fulfillment.

- *Feeling empty.* This usually happens for me when I'm not connected to Jesus, family, and/or friends.

Looking closely at the ways that regret, guilt, and emptiness pop up for you could help you zero in on what's truly important for your sense of fulfillment.

So, what are your ingredients and warning signs?

---

PRACTICE THE SKILL
## Learn Your Ingredients for Day-to-Day Fulfillment

1. *Assess.* Dedicate time to walk through these questions:

- What are your primary roles in life (friend, family member, child of God, worker, writer, learner, creative person . . .)?
- What brings you day-to-day fulfillment in your different roles?
- Lack of what starts to wear on you over time?
- What short-term preferences are getting in the way of fulfillment for you?

2. *Isolate your ingredients for day-to-day fulfillment.*

- What are you willing to do less of to create space for more fulfilling experiences?
- What are two to three fulfilling activities you want to prioritize?
- Write down your intention: "I will do less of _____ for the sake of more _____." (Examples: "I will watch less Netflix in the evenings for the sake of more connection with my roommates," or "I will spend less

185

time on social media for the sake of time with God," or "I will choose what my grandma prefers for the sake of our relationship.")

3. *Dig deeper.*

- How do your life and schedule support some of these decisions well?
- What will get in the way of your intention? What are you willing to do about it?
- What small tweaks could make a difference?

4. *Implement.*

- Schedule time for the things that require it. Write them on your calendar.
- Set up reminders to help you stick to your commitment.

After many small yet substantial tweaks and several weeks of effort, Jorge feels different. We started with applying focused work and the phone pickup challenge. After that, he built in a daily check-in time with his wife. They started with fifteen minutes, but it was often going longer many times per week. Jorge and his wife then decided to have a family game night once a week, and he started taking over the bedtime routine on half the nights. He also returned to a monthly meeting of three old friends who gathered to share with and pray for each other (he'd stopped attending after his third child was born). Reconnecting with them has meant that a happy, humorous text stream has become part of his near-daily life, with the friends regularly sending each other amusing memes and article links. More recently, Jorge has decided to go into the office one hour earlier twice weekly for some quiet time to think deeply about his work—long-term planning, projects, and less-urgent matters. Meanwhile, he's been slowly trying to build a rhythm of journaling and prayer into two other mornings per week. I ask him what he's been noticing.

Jorge's hair flops over his eyes as he presses his chin into his hand to think. After a moment, he looks up and says, "The biggest thing is that I feel more connected: to God, my kids, my wife, my friends . . . but mostly to myself, I think."

I feel a smile pulling at my mouth. "Oh, cool! Say more."

Jorge's eyes wander as he looks for a way to explain. "Before we started 'Project Fulfillment' [he adds air quotes, which makes me chuckle], I felt like I couldn't grab on to anything. Nothing was ever finished or satisfying. I felt so irritated with my kids all the time, even though they didn't do anything! I just kept seeing them as hindrances."

He pauses, blinking quickly. "Now, no matter what may still be lingering from work, I know that when I'm with them, I'm with them. Same with my wife. Before, I never felt like I could do that because the rest of the day had been such a disaster. Now I frequently leave work with that confident, satisfied feeling you were talking about. All that's different is that I get done what I've set out to do!"

I'm really smiling now. "You said you now feel connected to yourself. Can you expand on that?"

Nodding, Jorge starts slowly: "This sounds so lame, but I feel like I'm being who I'm supposed to be. Like this is *me*—the real me. And that I'm living the life God has given me to live. You were right; I didn't need a big career change. I just needed to figure out how to live in the one I have. I mean, not that I have it all figured out, but so much feels different."

"That's not lame. In fact, it's quite the opposite. Jorge, you are well on your way to the rich and satisfying life that Jesus has in mind for you."

• ● ● ●  •

Jesus wants us to live lives that are rich and satisfying—in our moments and days, in seasons of blessing and seasons of hardship. It is doable. It is possible. Your life can be more fulfilling. Don't shortchange the skills in this chapter. I encourage you to return to them regularly because momentum pulls us back to less-fulfilling behaviors if we aren't vigilant. Don't underestimate the gravitational pull of phones or the impact of the constant messaging from society. Remember that the thief won't stop trying to steal, kill, and destroy fulfillment in your life. Without intentional, regular effort, we'll wind up sliding into old patterns. And examining fulfillment requires thoughtful, periodic attending. Life alters, relationships shift, and priorities change, and we need to retool our efforts accordingly. I've never regretted putting in the work, and I believe it'll be worth the effort for you. Don't let another week go by with your soul suffering from empty days. The very best self-care is here for you. It's yours for the taking.

# Gratitudes

I'm so grateful for my family, my small group, my glitters, and all of you in my tribe who have cheered me on and encouraged me at key points along the way.

Special thanks to Dan, who built many "writer's fires" to warm me as I worked and brought me countless cups of coffee to keep my brain going. I love the life we share, encouraging each other in the various ways we pursue our call to follow Jesus.

My wonderful children, Brenna and Owen: You have shaped me in every way possible, and I am so grateful for you! Our COVID pod was a warm and encouraging space while I was writing this book.

For my friend Susie, who read and edited every word of this book with her brilliant lawyer brain before it went to the publisher. Thank you for taking time to think so deeply with me about this project. There aren't enough words to adequately thank you . . .

For Úna and Katie, who read chapters and gave me key feedback, who encouraged me, prayed for me, and challenged me to keep going at key points. This book may not have gotten finished without you.

For Deborah Gonzalez, my editor at NavPress, thank you for thoughtful affirmations and grounding conversations that helped me stay steady along the way.

For Cindy Bunch, who helped me reconceive the whole book to give it a more encouraging tone.

Thank you to my friends in the Couples Institute Mentor Program. You've all been cheering me on, and several of you have also been keeping me on task. I'm grateful for my tribe, who sharpens me and presses me to believe that my work ought to be out in the world in a bigger way.

I'm grateful for my clients, who trust me with their stories and who have become so, so dear. Our work together over the years is the backdrop for this book. Many of you worked with me as I was experimenting with and shaping the concepts found here. The change in *your* lives has encouraged and shaped me! It's because of you all that I've been able to shape my life around the work of restoring souls, and I couldn't be more appreciative.

For the people who have attended my workshops and conferences, where many of the ideas in this book were challenged and wrestled with. Thank you for your energy and responsiveness. It fueled me at many important points.

I'm so grateful for my key teachers and mentors along the way. Carl Robbins, you hired me and changed my life. I'm so grateful for your depth of wisdom in dealing with one's inner experiences. For my spiritual directors, who have shaped me and created sacred space for me: Mark Phifer-Houseman, Sister Connie Fitzgerald, Marilyn Stewart, and Marilyn Vancil. For Suzanne Stabile, Jerome Wagner, and Richard Rohr (and so many others), who, through their teachings and training, helped me bring together Enneagram wisdom and the ideas in this book.

For my beloved pets. Nala, my puppy: As much as it annoyed me at the time, your waking me up at 5:30 a.m. for nearly a year helped this book get written. Duffy and Zelda: Your cuddles all around me and my computer warmed me and made me laugh.

And finally, for Jesus, my Good Shepherd, who wants me to have a rich and satisfying life.

# Soul Restoration
# by Enneagram Type

As an Enneagram Type 4, it isn't uncommon that I find myself in an emotionally swirly hot mess of despair. Almost anything can spark it: an upcoming speaking event, being left out of a social gathering, or perceiving that a family member is disappointed with me. It starts with feeling some big emotion (nervousness, hurt, uncertainty). Then I start thinking about it, trying to work it out in my mind, which raises more feelings, which sparks more thoughts, which churns the feelings—and on and on I go. I can get stuck in this swirly place for a long, long time if I don't wake up and apply intentional *doing* in my life. *Doing* involves shifting my energy away from my internal tumult and toward something outside myself. It could be doing something mundane, like putting away laundry or picking up dog food. Or it could be tackling a work task or reading something that pulls me outside myself. And it is usually good for me to make plans with a friend while I'm in this state.

Most people who are familiar with the Enneagram have a basic understanding of the nine types, but not everyone is aware that knowledge of this system can go much deeper. Suzanne Stabile's training on stances and repressed centers was an "aha!" moment for me because it helped me understand the way people fall into their own stuck places based on their type. I highly recommend her workshop on this (#GoDeeper with the Enneagram) and her book *The Journey toward Wholeness* if you desire to take your Enneagram study to the next level. My purpose for this appendix is to provide a summary of the stances and repressed centers so that those of you who utilize this system's wisdom can integrate this into what you've learned from my book.

The Enneagram types are divided into three centers of intelligence, or triads:

- the heart center (Types 2, 3, and 4),
- the head center (Types 5, 6, and 7), and
- the gut center (Types 8, 9, and 1).

According to Stabile, "Your triad is determined by your first response when you encounter information or situations—with either feeling, thinking, or doing."[1] So the heart types respond to situations initially by asking how they feel; the head types, by determining what they think; and the gut types by wondering what they will do. Each triad represents the *dominant* center for its corresponding Enneagram types. So, each of us has a dominant center, but the other two centers are also present within us. One of them supports our dominant center, but the other is considered *repressed* in each of us, meaning that we must work intentionally to bring our repressed center forward and learn to utilize it to find balance and grow toward wholeness.

I have learned from various resources[2] that, depending on our Enneagram type, we tend to move in one of three directions when we encounter others:

- away from other people—**withdrawing** types (4, 5, and 9);
- toward other people—**dependent** types (1, 2, and 6); or
- against (or independent of[3]) other people—**aggressive** types (3, 7, and 8).

For the Enneagram enthusiasts who are reading this appendix: This means there are three additional categories of interest in Enneagram wisdom, which we call the *stances*. Each stance has a repressed center:

- withdrawing types repress *doing*,
- dependent types repress *thinking*, and
- aggressive types repress *feeling*.

So for myself, as an Enneagram 4 in the withdrawing stance, my dominant center is feeling, and the thinking center in me supports my feeling center. Thus the loop I described—feel, then think, then feel, then think . . . et cetera. Without intentional effort, I'm prone to stay there a *very* long time. To have balance, I need to employ helpful *doing*, both in the moments when big emotions hit me and in the day-to-day mundane efforts to care for myself and make life work.

Stabile explains further:

> By repressed, I don't mean that the center is unused or weak, just that it is underused in comparison to the other two centers. That's why people who have repressed thinking can have multiple degrees but not think productively. People who repress feeling can have lots of successful relationships but not know what they themselves truly feel. And people who repress doing can responsibly manage their jobs with great efficiency but may not always do the right thing.[4]

It would be inaccurate, therefore, to say that people with repressed thinking, feeling, or doing neglect to think, feel, or do. But often their efforts in their repressed center need refining.

As I wrote this book, I intuitively knew that some readers would likely identify their greatest need for help in certain chapters more than others. Some people would benefit more from working with their thoughts, others would resonate more with the need to identify and accept their emotions, and others would figure out the best kinds of "doing" to add to their lives to feel and live better. The wisdom of the Enneagram stances helps fill this out quite well!

## Enneagram Types 4, 5, and 9

If you are an Enneagram Type 4, 5, or 9, this means you are in the withdrawing stance with repressed *doing*. You will find life-giving help in the rhythms and fulfillment chapters that you can practice to find your way out of the internal swirls. I hope that you find at least one concrete thing to *do* that pulls you out of the paralysis of not knowing which action of the many choices before you will be truly helpful. There are so many ideas that you can try from these chapters that cross the range from small or occasional to significant and daily. But experiment with several of the ideas! By integrating *doing* ideas like these, you stretch the part that isn't as accessible to you.

## Enneagram Types 1, 2, and 6

If you are an Enneagram Type 1, 2, or 6, this means you are in the dependent stance with repressed *thinking*. Please know that I am not assuming that you don't think! Most people in this stance report that they think nearly constantly! But the work in your repressed center has to do with learning to do *different* thinking. The chapters on thinking are written to help you do exactly that: less unhelpful and more helpful thinking. The skills presented in these pages represent tried-and-true practices that have changed the lives of many of my clients who are in this stance. Recognizing thinking patterns is the first step.

## Enneagram Types 3, 7, and 8

Finally, for those who are an Enneagram Type 3, 7, or 8, you are in the aggressive stance with repressed *feeling*. I know that you feel many emotions, but you may find them difficult to admit, name, or respond well to. The emotions chapters are the place where I offer suggestions to help you grow in all these capacities. The church has not always been helpful in its messaging regarding emotions, so the confusion about how to wield them is real! I hope that by diving into these chapters, you'll find your way to greater emotional health and overall well-being.

⬤ ⬤ ⬤ ⬤ ⬤

It is my prayer that this book in your hands helps you move toward meaningful self-care and soul-restoring work. And for all my fellow Ennea-geeks out there, I hope that this volume finds its way to your Enneagram book collection as a resource that you return to for further sharpening and fresh ideas as you need them along the way. To experience growth in our repressed centers, each of us must do ongoing work, and we will slide back toward the pull of our dominant center without intentional effort. I hope that this book will be a blessing and help as you resist that pull and stretch yourself into utilizing your repressed centers more often. Bless you in the journey!

# Notes

## INTRODUCTION

1. W. Phillip Keller, *A Shepherd Looks at Psalm 23* (Grand Rapids, MI: Zondervan, 2007), 70.
2. See also Suzanne Stabile, *The Journey Toward Wholeness: Enneagram Wisdom for Stress, Balance, and Transformation* (Downers Grove, IL: InterVarsity Press, 2021).
3. Suzanne Stabile's books and workshops can be found at lifeinthetrinityministry.com/store.

## CHAPTER ONE | REIMAGINING SELF-CARE

1. Ashley Oerman, "Barbie Is Doing 'Self-Care' Now, and I Think We've Gone Too Far," *Cosmopolitan*, January 30, 2020, https://www.cosmopolitan.com/health-fitness/a30718416/wellness-barbie-mattel.

## CHAPTER TWO | LIVING WELL WITH OUR THOUGHTS

1. B. Grace Bullock, "Present-Moment Awareness Buffers the Effects of Daily Stress," Mindful.org, March 15, 2017, https://www.mindful.org/present-moment-awareness-buffers-effects-daily-stress.
2. Silvia Pittman, "New Study Suggests People Have More than 6,000 Thoughts Per Day," The Mighty, July 15, 2020, https://themighty.com/2020/07/study-how-many-thoughts-per-day.
3. Dallas Willard, *Renovation of the Heart: Putting on the Character of Christ*, 20th anniv. ed. (Colorado Springs: NavPress, 2021), 95.
4. Philippians 2:28, NIV (emphasis added).
5. Demi Lovato, "Confident," *Confident* © 2015 Hollywood Records; Archie Eversole, "We Ready," *Ride Wit Me Dirty South Style* © 2001 Phat Boy Records.

## CHAPTER THREE | THOUGHTS: THE ESSENTIAL SKILLS

1. Mark Phifer-Houseman.
2. Matthew 6:27, author's paraphrase.
3. I learned this metaphor during my training with Carl Robbins and Sally Winston at the Anxiety and Stress Disorders Institute.

## CHAPTER FOUR | LIVING WELL WITH OUR EMOTIONS

1. Jill Bolte Taylor, *Whole Brain Living: The Anatomy of Choice and the Four Characters That Drive Our Life* (Carlsbad, CA: Hay House, 2021), 7.
2. Ephesians 4:26, NIV.
3. William Barclay, *The Gospel of John*, vol. 2, rev. ed., The Daily Study Bible Series (Philadelphia: Westminster Press, 1977), 98–100.

## CHAPTER FIVE | EMOTIONS: THE ESSENTIAL SKILLS

1. See Christina Congleton, Britta K. Hölzel, and Sara W. Lazar, "Mindfulness Can Literally Change Your Brain," *Harvard Business Review*, January 8, 2015, https://hbr.org/2015/01/mindfulness-can-literally-change-your-brain and Ruth Graham, "This Is Your Brain on Faith," *US Catholic*, June 10, 2014, https://uscatholic.org/articles/201406/this-is-your-brain-on-faith.
2. Dee Wagner, "Polyvagal Theory in Practice," *Counseling Today*, June 27, 2016, https://ct.counseling.org/2016/06/polyvagal-theory-practice.

## CHAPTER SEVEN | RHYTHMS: THE ESSENTIAL SKILLS

1. For an overview of the function and history of praying the hours, see britannica.com/topic/divine-office. For a guide to praying the hours, see bcponline.org.
2. For more on the Examen, see ignatianspirituality.com/ignatian-prayer/the-examen.
3. For an evening prayer, see northumbriacommunity.org/offices/evening-prayer.
4. Make sure to compensate by drinking more water earlier in the day to stay adequately hydrated.
5. Talk to your doctor. You may benefit from a referral to a sleep specialist.
6. Emily Nagoski and Amelia Nagoski, *Burnout: The Secret to Unlocking the Stress Cycle* (New York: Ballantine Books, 2019), 4–8.
7. Nagoski and Nagoski, *Burnout*, 8.

## CHAPTER EIGHT | LIVING A LIFE OF FULFILLMENT

1. Michael W. Anderson and Timothy D. Johanson, *Gist: The Essence of Raising Life-Ready Kids* (Colorado Springs: Focus on the Family, 2019), 62.

## CHAPTER NINE | FULFILLMENT: THE ESSENTIAL SKILLS

1. Trevor Wheelwright, "2022 Cell Phone Usage Statistics: How Obsessed Are We?," Reviews.org, January 24, 2022, https://www.reviews.org/mobile/cell-phone-addiction.
2. For many of us, this is via our phones. Andrew Perrin and Sara Atske, "About Three-in-Ten U.S. Adults Say They Are 'Almost Constantly' Online," Pew Research Center, March 26, 2021, https://www.pewresearch.org/fact-tank/2021/03/26/about-three-in-ten-u-s-adults-say-they-are-almost-constantly-online.
3. "Phone Addiction: Warning Signs and Treatment," Addiction Center, accessed February 2, 2022, https://www.addictioncenter.com/drugs/phone-addiction.

4. Tony Schwartz, "Addicted to Distraction," *New York Times*, November 28, 2015, https://www.nytimes.com/2015/11/29/opinion/sunday/addicted-to-distraction.html.

5. I've been teaching clients this method for years. Recently, I learned that there's a similar strategy called the Pomodoro Technique. For more, see todoist.com/productivity-methods/pomodoro-technique.

6. The Gap Band, "You Dropped a Bomb on Me," *Gap Band IV*, Total Experience Records, 1982; KC and the Sunshine Band, "Boogie Shoes," *KC and the Sunshine Band*, TK Records, 1975; Earth, Wind & Fire, "Let's Groove," *Raise!*, Columbia, 1981.

## APPENDIX | SOUL RESTORATION BY ENNEAGRAM TYPE

1. Suzanne Stabile, *The Journey toward Wholeness: Enneagram Wisdom for Stress, Balance, and Transformation* (Downers Grove, IL: InterVarsity Press, 2021), 5.

2. Robert J. Nogosek, *The Enneagram Journey to New Life: Who Am I? What Do I Stand For?* (Denville, NJ: Dimension Books, 1995); Kathleen Hurley and Theodore E. Dobson, *My Best Self: Using the Enneagram to Free the Soul* (San Francisco: HarperSanFrancisco, 1993).

3. Suzanne Stabile has moved toward the idea of "standing independent of" instead of "against"; see Stabile, *Journey*, 135.

4. Stabile, *Journey*, 132.

# About the Author

Janice's first work as an author was in the journal she wrote that spanned her middle school years. That journal was filled with *intense* crushes (on people she can no longer remember), her *intense* feelings about, well, everything, and her *intense* desire to be seen and known. A closer read reveals her desire to understand how people work, and to find life's meaning.

That middle school exploration of the human experience led her quite naturally into the area of soul care as a profession—first in campus ministry with InterVarsity Christian Fellowship; then at Howard University School of Divinity, where she got an MDiv; then in Loyola University Maryland's pastoral counseling program; then in spiritual director training at the School for Spiritual Directors at the Monastery of the Risen Christ; and through several Enneagram trainings and eventual certification in the Enneagram Spectrum Training. Through these pursuits, Janice has been asking, *What makes people tick?* and *What blocks people from being the best version of themselves?* and *How can we learn from Jesus how to live?* Her passion throughout all these experiences has been empowering people—and herself—to find the answers to these questions. Nothing makes her happier than seeing people become able to enjoy life more and find their place in God's story.

Visit janicemcwilliams.com for more resources to help you in your journey.

**NavPress is the book-publishing arm of The Navigators.**

Since 1933, The Navigators has helped people around the world bring hope and purpose to others in college campuses, local churches, workplaces, neighborhoods, and hard-to-reach places all over the world, face-to-face and person-by-person in an approach we call Life-to-Life® discipleship. We have committed together to know Christ, make Him known, and help others do the same.®

Would you like to join this adventure of discipleship and disciplemaking?

- Take a Digital Discipleship Journey at **navigators.org/disciplemaking**.
- Get more discipleship and disciplemaking content at **thedisciplemaker.org**.
- Find your next book, Bible, or discipleship resource at **navpress.com**.

 @NavPressPublishing

 @NavPress

@navpressbooks

CP1790